GED
WRITING SKILLS
WORKBOOK

SHARON SORENSON
Writing Consultant

MACMILLAN • USA

Second Edition

Macmillan General Reference
A Simon & Schuster Macmillan Company
1633 Broadway
New York, NY 10019-6785

An Arco Book

MACMILLAN is a registered trademark of Macmillan, Inc.
ARCO is a registered trademark of Prentice-Hall, Inc.

Library of Congress Cataloging-in-Publication Data

Sorenson, Sharon.
  GED writing skills workbook / Sharon Sorenson.—2nd ed.
  p. cm.
  At head of title: Arco.
  Rev. ed. of: Writing skills workbook for the GED © 1991.
  ISBN 0-13-347188-8
   1. English language—composition and exercises—Examinations, questions, etc.
2. General educational development tests—Study guides. I. Sorenson, Sharon.
Writing skills workbook for the GED. II. Title. III. Title: Arco GED writing skills handbook.
LB1631.S657   1992   92-2639
428'.0076—dc20   CIP

Manufactured in the United States of America

10 9 8 7

CONTENTS

Introduction ix

Note to the Teacher x

I: Fundamentals

    1:    Classification of Words 3
        Part 1:   Nouns 3
        Part 2:   Verbs 5
        Part 3:   Adjectives 8
        Part 4:   Adverbs 10
        Part 5:   Prepositions 12

        Practice 14

    2:    Parts of the Sentence 18
        A Sentence-Attack Plan 18

        Step 1:   Prepositional Phrases 18
        Step 2:   Verbs 18
        Step 3:   Action Verb or Linking Verb 19
        Step 4:   Subjects 19
        Step 5:   Direct Objects 20
        Step 6:   Indirect Objects 21
        Step 7:   Objective Complements 23
        Step 8:   Predicate Words 23

        Compound Parts 24
        Summary of the Sentence-Attack Plan 25
        Practice 26

II: Usage

    3:    Agreement of Subject and Verb 35
        Basic Premises 35

        Problem 1: Choosing the Subject 36
        Problem 2: Indefinite Pronouns 37
        Problem 3: Compound Subjects 38
        Problem 4: Collective Nouns 39
        Problem 5: Nouns Plural in Form 40

        Practice 42

    4:    Pronoun Usage 46
        Rule 1:   Subject Pronouns 46
        Rule 2:   Pronouns as Predicate Words 46

		Rule 3:	Object Pronouns	47
		Rule 4:	Pronouns with Nouns	47
		Rule 5:	Pronouns in Comparison	47
		Rule 6:	Pronouns with *-ing* Words	48
		Rule 7:	Pronouns Used as Appositives	48
		Rule 8:	Compound Pronouns	49
		Rule 9:	Who/Whom	49
		Rule 10:	Agreement	50
		Practice		51
	5:	Adjective and Adverb Usage		55
		Rule 1:	Adverbs and Action Verbs	55
		Rule 2:	Adverbs with Adjectives	55
		Rule 3:	Adjectives with Linking Verbs	55
		Rule 4:	Bad/Badly	55
		Rule 5:	Good/Well	56
		Rule 6:	Fewer/Less	56
		Rule 7:	Comparatives and Superlatives	57
		Rule 8:	Double Negatives	57
		Rule 9:	Illogical Comparisons	57
		Practice		58
	6:	Troublesome Verbs		60
		Pair 1:	Sit/Set	60
		Pair 2:	Rise/Raise	60
		Pair 3:	Lie/Lay	61
		Summary		61
		Practice		62
III:	Phrases and Clauses			
	7:	Verbals		67
		Part 1:	Infinitives	67
		Part 2:	Gerunds	70
		Part 3:	Participles	72
		Practice		75
	8:	Clauses		76
		Part 1:	Noun Clause	76
		Part 2:	Adjective Clause	78
		Part 3:	Adverb Clause	80
		Practice		84
IV:	Punctuation			
	9:	Commas		89
		Rule 1:	Commas with a Series	89
		Rule 2:	Commas with Coordinate Adjectives	90
		Rule 3:	Commas with Compound Sentences	90

Rule 4:   Commas with Nonrestrictive Elements 91
Rule 5:   Commas with Introductory Elements 92
Rule 6:   Commas with Interrupters 93
Rule 7:   Commas with Dates and States 94

Summary for Using Commas 94
Practice 95

10:   Semicolons and Colons 96
Part 1:   Semicolons 96
Part 2:   Colons 97

Summary for Using Semicolons and Colons 99
Practice 100

11:   Other Punctuation 101
Part 1:   End Marks 101
Part 2:   Apostrophes 102
Part 3:   Italics 103
Part 4:   Quotation Marks 103
Part 5:   Multiple Punctuation Marks 104

Practice 105

12:   Capitalization 107
Rule 1:   First Words 107
Rule 2:   Titles 107
Rule 3:   Proper Names 108
Rule 4:   Salutations and Closings 108

Practice 109

13:   Commonly Confused Words 110
14:   GED Practice for Sections I to IV 114

V: Sentences

15:   Basic Sentence Structures 121
Part 1:   Simple Sentences 121
Part 2:   Compound Parts and Compound Sentences 122
            Compound Subjects 122
            Compound Verbs 123
            Compound Sentences 123
Part 3:   Complex Sentences 125
            Independent Clauses 125
            Dependent Clauses 126
            Joined Clauses 126
            Noun Clause 127
            Adjective Clause 127
            Adverb Clause 127
Part 4:   Compound-Complex Sentences 128

Practice 129

16: Common Sentence Problems 134
    Problem 1: Using Specific Words 134

    Identifying Vague Words 134
    Replacing Vague Words 135

    Problem 2: Combining Sentences 135
    Problem 3: Placing Words Correctly 137
    Problem 4: Balancing Sets of Words 137
    Problem 5: Avoiding Run-ons and Comma Splices 138
    Problem 6: Avoiding Sentence Fragments 138

    Practice 140

    Checklist for Writing Effective Sentences 145

VI: Paragraphs

17: Statement of Purpose 149
    Practice 151

18: Paragraph Contents 152
    Part 1: Using Specific Details 152
    Part 2: Putting Details in Order 153
            Time Order 153
            Space Order 154
            Orders of Importance 155
    Part 3: Using Connecting Words 158
    Part 4: Staying on the Subject 159

    Practice 160

19: Paragraph Accuracy 164
    Problem 1: Using Correct Verb Tense 164
            Using Simple Tenses 164
            Using Perfect Tenses 164
            Recognizing Progressive Form 165
            Showing Time Relationships 165
    Problem 2: Using One Point of View 166
            Identifying First-Person Point of View 166
            Identifying Second-Person Point of View 167
            Identifying Third-Person Point of View 167
            Choosing Point of View 168

    Practice 169

20: Conclusion 171
    Methods of Concluding 171
    Model Paragraph 172
    Practice 173

    Checklist for Writing Powerful Paragraphs 174

VII: Four Kinds of Essays

21: Explaining How 177
Organization 177
Model 178
Practice 180

Checklist for Writing a Paper That Explains How 181

22: Explaining Why 182
Organization 182
Models 183
Practice 186

Checklist for Writing a Paper That Explains Why 187

23: Stating and Supporting an Opinion 188
Organization 188
Model 189
Practice 191

Checklist for Writing an Opinion Paper 192

24: Showing Advantages and Disadvantages 193
Organization 193
Model 195
Practice 198

Checklist for an Advantages/Disadvantages Paper 199

25: GED Practice for Sections V to VII 200
Sample Practice Test 201

VIII: The GED Essay

26: Writing the GED Essay 207
Part 1: Planning Your Response 207
Part 2: Writing Your Essay 211
Part 3: Checking Your Essay 212

Model 213
Practice 214

BOOKS
FOR GED CANDIDATES

GED Preparation

GED: High School Equivalency Examination
GED en Español
GED Mathematics Workbook
GED Writing Skills Workbook

Resume Guides

The Complete Resume Guide
Resumes for Better Jobs
Resumes That Get Jobs
Your Resume: Key to a Better Job

Military

ASVAB: Practice for the Armed Forces Test
ASVAB Basics
Officer Candidate Tests
Military Flight Aptitude Tests
Military Life: The Insider's Guide

Careers / Study Guides

Business Typing
Civil Service Administrative Tests
Civil Service Arithmetic and Vocabulary
Civil Service Clerical Promotion Tests
Civil Service Handbook
Civil Service Psychological and Psychiatric
    Tests
Civil Service Reading Comprehension Tests
Civil Service Tests for Basic Skills Jobs
Complete Guide to U.S. Civil Service Jobs
General Test Practice for 101 U.S. Jobs
Homestudy Course for Civil Service Jobs
How to Get a Clerical Job in Government
How to Pass Civil Service Oral Examinations
New York City Civil Service Job Guide
101 Challenging Government Jobs for
    College Graduates
Practice for Clerical, Typing, and
    Stenographic Tests
SF 171: The Federal Employment
    Application Form
Supervision
Typing for Beginners
Typing for Everyone
You as a Law Enforcement Officer

AVAILABLE AT BOOKSTORES EVERYWHERE

PRENTICE HALL
Simon & Schuster / A Paramount Communications Company

INTRODUCTION

Congratulations! Taking this first step toward passing the GED test is indeed a big step—one that can lead to increased job potential and tremendous self-satisfaction.

This book is designed to help you succeed on the GED Writing Skills Test. As you probably know, the Writing Skills Test is in two parts, one part with multiple-choice questions and the other requiring an essay response. You must be successful with both parts in order to pass the test.

To help you, this practice book

—presents the subject matter you need to answer the multiple-choice questions
—includes subject-specific practice with every chapter
—offers GED practice material for the Writing Skills multiple-choice questions
—shows you how to prepare a successful essay response
—gives specific guidelines for writing the GED essay
—furnishes GED practice material for the essay response

As you work through the practice book, you will find cross references to remind you of things you already know. Be sure to check the references for review. The more carefully you practice, the more successful you will be on the test.

Best wishes to you. May you join the thousands before you who have found passing the GED test to be the stepping stone to new careers, new lives, and new personal satisfaction.

NOTE TO THE TEACHER

This practice book addresses both parts of the GED Writing Skills Test—the multiple-choice questions and the essay response. In Sections I to IV of the text, students study the rules and examples for grammar, usage, and mechanics. Practice follows each chapter. That portion of the practice book is followed by a sample GED application. Students are told that the GED test will not ask them to identify the parts of speech of all the words in a sentence or underline phrases or identify the kinds of clauses in a sentence. Rather, the test will ask them to *apply* their understanding of the rules in order to correct sentence errors. Answers to practice questions include an explanation for both the correct and the incorrect responses, with references to specific chapters and rules. The references permit students to review topics that are still causing difficulty.

In Sections V to VII students study how to write effective essays, especially the kinds of essays that generally appear on the GED test. The models for each kind of essay include marginal notes pointing out specific components of an effective essay. Research shows that careful study of models and their analyses is the most effective instructional technique for GED preparation. In addition, that portion of the practice book is also followed by a sample GED application.

The book concludes with a chapter that walks students through a sample GED essay question, from the planning stage to the completed essay, with marginal notes analyzing the completed essay response. Step-by-step suggestions show students how to plan, write, and check the essay response. The hints include suggestions on how to allot the forty-five-minute time limit most effectively and how to remember important points to check.

Now, for the first time, you can find in one text everything you need to help your students prepare for the GED Writing Skills Test.

I

FUNDAMENTALS

1

CLASSIFICATION OF WORDS

PART 1: NOUNS

A. Definition: A noun is the name of a person, place, or thing. Sometimes a substitute-name, called a pronoun, names the person, place, or thing. (But this traditional definition is not always adequate.)

> EXAMPLE: *Singing* in the *shower* is not for *me*.
> (*Singing* is the name of a thing; *shower* is the name of a place; and *me* is the substitute-name of a person.)

Often, definition alone is not sufficient to determine part of speech accurately. For instance, you may have looked at *singing* in the sentence above and thought at first that it looked like a verb. Without considering *function*, you may not recognize all nouns.

B. Function: A noun most commonly functions in one of three ways:

1. As the subject of a verb

> EXAMPLE: Some *elephants* dance.
> (*Elephants,* a noun, is subject of the verb *dance.*)

2. As an object

   a. As direct object of the verb

   > EXAMPLE: One elephant danced a *jig*.
   > (*Jig,* a noun, is the direct object of the verb *danced.*)

   b. As an indirect object of the verb

   > EXAMPLE: The trainer gave the *elephant* an apple.
   > (*Elephant,* a noun, is now the indirect object of the verb *gave.*)

   c. As object of the preposition

   > EXAMPLE: The elephant danced another jig for *me*.
   > (*Me,* a substitute-name, or pronoun, is the object of the preposition *for.*)

3

    d. As object of a verbal

        EXAMPLE: The elephant liked dancing *jigs*.
                     (*Jigs*, a noun, is the object of *dancing*.)

  3. As a predicate word

        EXAMPLE: The elephant is a *dancer*.
                     (*Dancer*, a noun, is the predicate noun after the linking verb *is*.)

Perhaps you are saying by now that you do not understand enough about such things as *direct objects* and *objects of verbals* (topics discussed in later chapters) for function to help you determine parts of speech. Later, however, when you have studied Chapter 2, you may come back and review function for additional clarity. These two chapters work hand-in-hand.

For now, though, however limited your understanding may be at this point concerning function, you will want also to consider noun *characteristics*.

  C. Characteristics: A noun may have the following characteristics that will help you distinguish it from other parts of speech. Not all nouns will have every one of the following characteristics.

    1. Certain endings indicate nouns:

      a. Nouns can be made plural, usually by adding -*s* or -*es*.

        EXAMPLES: elephant, elephant*s*; trainer, trainer*s*; circus, circus*es*

        NOTE: Some nouns have peculiar plural forms, like *child, children; goose, geese; he, they;* but most nouns can be made plural.

      b. Nouns can be made possessive by adding either an apostrophe and -*s* or an apostrophe only. When the noun is possessive, it functions as an *adjective*.

        EXAMPLES: tree, tree*'s* leaves; leaves, leave*s'* colors

    2. Certain words often appear in front of nouns:

      a. Articles: *a, an,* and *the*

        EXAMPLES: *the* tree, *a* tree, *an* earring, *a* ruby earring

        NOTE: For every article appearing in a sentence, there will be a noun following, although that noun may not be the very next word.

      b. Adjectives (words that describe shape, size, appearance, or number)

        EXAMPLES: *tall, cone-shaped* tree (describes size and shape of tree)
                     three golden maple trees (describes number, kind and appearance of trees)

In other words, certain characteristics will serve as a test to determine whether or not a word is a noun. If that word can be made plural (you can count them), or if that word can show ownership, or if that word can have *a, an, or the* in front, you can bet it will be a noun.

Look at the following nonsense sentence:

When the <u>jibjam</u> quots the <u>flitstat</u> after a <u>purdletroe</u> warkled the clatterstrow, the <u>barmel</u> praesslebrow was strottled by an <u>ubby</u> warkened.

Certain words in the sentence above are obviously nouns. Can you recognize them? Consider *characteristics*. Find all the articles (*a, an,* and *the*). You know that a noun has to follow an article, although maybe not immediately. (There may be an adjective or two between the article and the noun.) If you still do not know whether or not a word is a noun, check for plural forms. Then consider *function*. When you think you have found all the nouns, check your answers with those below.

Nouns in the nonsense sentence:

jibjam (*The* appears in front, and it is the subject of the verb *quots*.)
flitstat (*The* appears in front, and it is the direct object of the verb *quots*.)
purdletroe (*A* appears in front, and it is the subject of the verb *warkled*.)
clatterstrow (It is the direct object of *warkled*.)
praesslebrow (*The,* as well as the adjective *barmel,* appears in front, and it is the subject of the verb *strottled*.)
warkened (*An,* as well as the adjective *ubby,* appears in front, and it is the object of the preposition *by*.)

PART 2: VERBS

A. **Definition:** A verb shows action or state of being. This definition itself indicates that there are two kinds of verbs. As a result, there are also two basic functions:

B. **Function:**

1. Some verbs show action.

   EXAMPLE: Some students *chatter* constantly.
   (*Chatter* shows an action that the students are doing.)

2. Some verbs link the subject to the predicate word.

   EXAMPLE 1: Some students *are* noisy.
   (*Are* is a state of being or linking verb and links *students* to *noisy*. *Noisy* describes *students*. *Noisy* is a predicate adjective.)
   EXAMPLE 2: These young men and women *are* students.
   (*Are* now links *men* and *women* with *students*. *Students* renames *men* and *women*. *Students* is a predicate noun.)

Because verbs and verbals look so much alike, sometimes it is difficult to determine part of speech when one knows only definition and function. *Characteristics* will help you separate verbs from verbals.

C. **Characteristics:** Verbs show the following characteristics:

1. A verb changes time (or *tense*).
   To test for a verb, insert the words *yesterday* or *tomorrow* in front of the sentence. The word that changes is the verb.

EXAMPLE: They were singing in three-part harmony.
Yesterday, they were singing in three-part harmony. (no change)
Yesterday, they sang in three-part harmony.
Tomorrow, they will sing in three-part harmony.

From this simple test, you know that the word that changed, *were singing,* is the verb.

NOTE: You will often need to try *both yesterday* and *tomorrow* if you do not know in which time (or tense) the sentence is written.

a. Because a verb changes time, it has certain endings: *-s, -ed, -en, -ing*.

EXAMPLES: The bear *ambles* along the path.
The bear *ambled* along the path.
The bear *will amble* along the path.
The bear *is ambling* along the path.

☞   Hint: Do not confuse the *-s* ending on verbs with the *-s* ending on nouns. We add an *-s* to *nouns* to make them *plural;* we add an *-s* to *verbs* to make them *singular*.

EXAMPLES: The bears (plural *noun*) amble (plural *verb*).
The bear (singular *noun*) ambles (singular *verb*).

b. Because a verb changes time, it also may have certain helping verbs (or *auxiliaries*):

do	have	could	may	will
does	has	would	might	shall
did	had	should	must	

is	was	be
am	were	been
are		being

NOTE: The helper plus the main verb equals the complete verb phrase:

helper(s) + main verb = complete verb phrase

$$\left. \begin{array}{c} could \\ + \\ have \\ + \\ been \end{array} \right\} + spanked = \text{could have been spanked}$$

Some of the helping verbs can be used alone as main verbs; but when they appear with other verbs after them, they are helpers.

EXAMPLE 1:   Marty and Jo have their homework.
(*Have* is the entire verb.)
EXAMPLE 2:   Marty and Jo *should* have their homework.
(*Should* is a helper for the main verb *have*.)

EXAMPLE 3: Marty and Jo *have finished* their homework.
(*Have* is a helper for the main verb *finished; finished* appears after *have.*)

EXAMPLE 4: Gerry *should have finished* her homework.
(*Should* and *have* are both helpers; *finished* appears after *have* and *should* and therefore is the main verb.)

NOTE: The verb that appears *last* in the verb phrase is the main verb.

So the first characteristic of a verb is that it changes time. Now you are ready for the second and third characteristics:

2. Most verbs show action.

   a. The subject does something. (The verb is in active voice.)

   EXAMPLE: That boy *ate* a grasshopper!

   b. The subject has something done to it. (The verb is in passive voice.)

   EXAMPLE: The grasshopper *was eaten* by that boy.

3. Some verbs are linking. There are two kinds of linking verbs:

   a. Verbs that are always linking verbs:

is	was	be
am	were	been
are		being

   NOTE: These verbs are always linking when they are the *main* verbs. If they are merely *helping* verbs, they are *not* linking.

   EXAMPLE 1: She *could have been* a beautiful girl.
   (*Been* is the main verb, so the verb is linking.)

   EXAMPLE 2: Linda is *being treated* for a serious illness.
   (*Is* and *being* are only helpers for the main verb *treated,* so the verb is action, not linking.)

   b. Verbs that can be linking verbs or action verbs:

seem	appear	remain
become	grow	stay

   look ⎫
   smell ⎪
   taste ⎬ verbs of the senses
   sound ⎪
   feel ⎭

The trick of it, of course, is to be able to recognize when these verbs are action verbs and when they are linking verbs.

To Check: Substitute some form of *to be* (*is, am, are, was, were, be, been,* or *being*) for any one of these eleven verbs. If the substitution makes sense, that verb is linking.

EXAMPLE 1: He *felt* miserable.
He *was* miserable.
(A form of *to be* works, so *felt* is a linking verb.)

EXAMPLE 2: She *felt* the fabric.
She *was* the fabric.
(No! *Felt* in this sentence is *not* a linking verb.)

EXAMPLE 3: He *tasted* the cake.
He *was* the cake.
(No! *Tasted* here is *not* a linking verb.)

EXAMPLE 4: The cake *tasted* delicious.
The cake *was* delicious.
(A form of *to be* works, so *tasted* is a linking verb.)

⇨ Warning: Be aware that a form of *to be* can substitute for other verbs that will *not* be linking:

EXAMPLE: The pictures *hung* on the wall.
The pictures *were* on the wall.

But *hung* is *not* a linking verb. It is not one of the eleven verbs listed in (b) above.

When words like *hung* appear in a sentence, you may wish to check your dictionary to see whether or not the verb can function as a linking verb.

Sometimes, it is difficult to know whether the verb is a linking verb followed by a predicate word or if the verb is, in fact, a verb phrase.

EXAMPLES: The author was dedicated to his work.
The book was dedicated to the author's students.
The author is dedicating the book to her students.

In the first sentence, *was* is the linking verb, and *dedicated* is a predicate adjective. In the second sentence, the verb is *was dedicated.* In the third sentence, the verb is *is dedicating.* How can you tell? Where there is some form of *to be* (*is, am, are, was, were, be, been,* or *being*) plus another word that looks like a verb, insert the word *very* after the verb *to be.* If *very* makes sense, the verb is a linking verb with a predicate word. If *very* does *not* make sense, then you have a verb phrase.

EXAMPLE 1: The author was [very] dedicated to his work.
(Because *very* works here, you know that *was* is a linking verb.)

EXAMPLE 2: The book was [very] dedicated to the author's students.
(Because *very* does not make sense, you know the verb phrase is *was dedicated.*)

EXAMPLE 3: The author is [very] dedicating the book to her students.
(*Very* does not work; the verb phrase is *is dedicating.*)

PART 3: ADJECTIVES

A. Definition: An adjective describes or modifies a noun.

B. Function: An adjective will answer one of these questions about a noun:

1. *Which one?*

   EXAMPLE: The *broken* chair was in the *south* hall.
   (*Broken* describes which *chair*, and *south* tells which *hall*.)

2. *What kind?*

   EXAMPLE: Her *wool* sweater kept out the *biting* cold.
   (*Wool* describes what kind of *sweater*, and *biting* describes what kind of *cold*.)

3. *How many?*

   EXAMPLE: *Seven* students attended the meeting.
   (*Seven* tells how many *students*.)

4. *Whose?*

   EXAMPLE: The *student's* chair was outside *her* door.
   (*Student's* describes whose *chair*, and *her* describes whose *door*.)

Remember that one of the characteristics of a noun is that adjectives can appear in front of it. This means that each of the words being described above is a noun:

   the *broken* (adjective) *chair* (noun)
   the *south* (adjective) *hall* (noun)
   the *wool* (adjective) *sweater* (noun)
   the *biting* (adjective) *cold* (noun)
   seven (adjective) *students* (noun)
   the *student's* (adjective) *chair* (noun)
   her (adjective) *door* (noun)

Recognizing adjectives will help you recognize nouns—and vice-versa! Finally, you will want to recognize the adjectives' characteristics.

C. Characteristics:

1. Certain endings on adjectives enable us to make comparisons.

   EXAMPLE 1: Andrea is a *brave* girl.
   (We are talking about only one girl, so we use the plain form of the adjective, *brave*.)
   EXAMPLE 2: Betty, however, is *braver* than Andrea.
   (Now we are talking about the comparison of two girls, so we use the comparative form, the *-er* form, *braver*.)
   EXAMPLE 3: But Priscilla is the *bravest* of the three.
   (Since we are now comparing three, we must use the superlative form, the *-est* form, *bravest*.)

We often misuse these three forms—usually substituting the *-est* form for the *-er* form. For instance, if you have only one brother and he is taller than you, then he is the *taller* of the two; you are the *shorter* (not *shortest*). If you have a sister two years younger than you and you have no other brothers or sisters, then you are the *older* child (not *oldest*) in your family. If, on the other hand, you have *two* siblings, both of whom are older than you, then you are the *youngest* of the three. To summarize:

one person	= brave, short, old, young
one of *two* persons	= braver, shorter, older, younger
one of *three* or more persons	= bravest, shortest, oldest, youngest

The endings *-er* and *-est* will work for short adjectives, but if the adjective has three or more syllables, use another word instead of the ending:

brave	brav|er|	brave|st|
beautiful	mo|re| beautiful	mo|st| beautiful

Use *more* like *-er* and *most* like *-est*.

Of course, there are some words that have their own peculiar comparisons, but you are no doubt familiar with them. You would not say *good, gooder, goodest,* now, would you! So you recognize *good, better,* and *best* as the usual comparisons. But the point remains: comparisons are characteristic of adjectives.

2. Placement also helps to identify adjectives.

   a. Adjectives usually appear in front of the nouns they modify.

      EXAMPLE: The *brave* girl rescued the kitten from the tree.
                (*Brave* describes *what kind* about the noun *girl*.)

   b. The adjective can appear after a linking verb. That adjective is called a predicate adjective.

      EXAMPLE: She is *brave*.
                (*Brave* describes *what kind* about the noun *she* and comes after the linking verb *is*.)

PART 4: ADVERBS

A. **Definition:** An adverb modifies a verb, an adjective, or another adverb.

B. **Function:** An adverb will answer the following questions about verbs, adjectives, or other adverbs:

   1. Where?

      EXAMPLE 1: He walked *home*.
                  (*Home* tells *where* about the verb *walked*.)
      EXAMPLE 2: The lumberjack cut *down* the tree.
                  (*Down* tells *where* about the verb *cut*. That sentence could also read this way: The lumberjack cut the tree *down*. Adverbs are movable!)

☞ Hint: Since adverbs are movable, try that moving test when you do not know whether *down* is an adverb or a preposition. Prepositions cannot be moved.

EXAMPLE 1: The fireman ran *down* the hall.
(Since we cannot say, "The fireman ran the hall down," we know that *down* is a preposition.)

EXAMPLE 2: The wrestler knocked *down* his opponent.
(We can say, "The wrestler knocked his opponent down," so we know the movable word is an adverb, not a preposition.)

2. When?

EXAMPLE 1: He walked to school *yesterday.*
(*Yesterday* tells *when* about the verb *walked.*)

EXAMPLE 2: The bell rang *late.*
(*Late* tells when about the verb *rang.*)

3. How?

EXAMPLE 1: The aspen swayed *gently* in the wind.
(*Gently* tells *how* about the verb *swayed.*)

EXAMPLE 2: The aspen swayed *very gently* in the wind.
(*Very* tells *how* about the adverb *gently.*)

4. To what extent?

EXAMPLE 1: He tried *quite* hard to finish the job.
(*Quite* tells *to what extent* about the adverb *hard. Hard* tells *how* about the verb *tried.*)

EXAMPLE 2: He was *absolutely* certain about the answer.
(*Absolutely* tells *to what extent* about the predicate adjective *certain.*)

C. **Characteristics:** Adverbs have two characteristic endings that help identify them:

1. Adverbs, like adjectives, can be compared using the endings *-er* and *-est* or the words *more* and *most.*

EXAMPLE 1: The men work *hard.*
EXAMPLE 2: The men worked *harder* today than they did yesterday.
(Comparison of how *hard* the men worked on *two* days requires the comparative, or *-er*, form.)
EXAMPLE 3: Of all the days in the week that they worked, the men worked *hardest* on Saturday.
(The comparison of how *hard* the men worked on six days requires the superlative *-est* form.)
EXAMPLE 4: The children behaved *properly.*
EXAMPLE 5: These children behaved *more properly* than those.
(Comparison of how *two* groups behaved requires the comparative, or *more,* form.)
EXAMPLE 6: Of the three groups of children, the neighbor's children behaved *most properly.*
(The comparison of how *three* groups behaved requires the superlative *most* form.)

Since both adjectives and adverbs have the characteristic of comparison, you will have to go back to consider *function* to distinguish between the two. Adjectives will make comparisons about *nouns*. Adverbs will make comparisons about *verbs, adjectives,* and other *adverbs.*

Consider, too, this additional characteristic ending of adverbs:

2. Adverbs often end in *-ly.*

EXAMPLE: He worked rapid*ly,* ate hungri*ly,* and slept sound*ly.*

⇨ Warning: Not all words that end in *-ly* are adverbs. Some are adjectives. Be sure to check function.

EXAMPLE: He was a *friendly* man who had a *burly* physique.
(*Friendly* tells what kind of *man* [noun], and *burly* tells what kind of *physique* [noun], so both are adjectives by *function.*)

PART 5: PREPOSITIONS

A. Definition: A preposition shows the relationship of its object to another word in the sentence. (That definition probably does not help much, but don't give up yet!)

B. Function: The preposition, with its object, functions as a single word.

NOTE: To find the object of the preposition, ask *who?* or *what?* after the preposition.

EXAMPLE 1: The poodle frisked *through the room.*
Ask: through *what?*
Answer: through *the room*
(*Room* is the object of the preposition *through.* The preposition and its object form the prepositional phrase *through the room. Through* shows the relationship between the noun *room* and the verb *frisked.*)

EXAMPLE 2: The terrier barked at the *frisky little poodle.*
Ask: at *who* or at *what?*
Answer: at *the poodle*
(*Poodle* is the object of the preposition *at.* The prepositional phrase begins with the preposition and ends with its object: at (preposition) *the frisky little poodle* (object of the preposition). The phrase includes, therefore, any modifiers of the object. In the sentence above, *frisky* and *little* both modify *poodle* and so are part of the prepositional phrase.)

To summarize, then, the prepositional phrase functions as a single word. It functions in one of two ways:

1. As an adjective

EXAMPLE: The girl *with red hair* is my friend.
(*With* shows the relationship of *hair* to *girl,* and *with red hair* tells

which about the noun *girl*. The whole phrase *with red hair* functions as a single word, as an adjective modifying *girl*.)

2. As an adverb

EXAMPLE: The girl who fell *into the bucket* of wet cement needs a hose. (*Into* shows the relationship between *fell* and *bucket*. *Into the bucket* says *where* about *fell,* and the whole phrase functions as a single word, as an adverb modifying the verb *fell*. Incidentally, *of wet cement* functions as an adjective describing *what kind* about *bucket*.)

C. **Characteristics:** The following characteristics indicate prepositions:

1. A preposition will always be followed by an object, which must be a noun. (Remember, *all* objects are nouns.)

Since prepositions are rather peculiar words that we use frequently, you really need to be able to recognize them easily. Prepositional phrases cause all sorts of problems later if you fail to learn to recognize them. Since the definition does not really help to identify prepositions easily, think of this final characteristic, peculiar though it may be, as one that will help you find those prepositions easily:

2. A preposition is "any place a rat can run." (The preposition *of* is the only exception!)

Strange? Yes, but look at the following list of prepositions, written here with objects (forming prepositional phrases), to see how this strange idea works:

A rat can run **about** the room,
above the window,
or **across** your desk
any time **after** 8:00,
even **against** your wishes.
He can run **along** your foot,
among your books,
or **around** your shoulders
at an easy pace.
That same rat can run **before** your very eyes
or **behind** your back,
below the bookcase
or **beneath** the door.
He can run **beside** your notebook,
between your boots,
or **beyond** your reach
by the file cabinet.
This wily little rat can run **down** your arm
during coffee break
except on Saturdays and Sundays

for many hours
from now **until** 3:30!
He can also run **from** the exterminator
in a panic
into hiding
like a flash
of lightning.
He can run **off** the window ledge
on the east side **of** the room,
over the wall,
through the meadow and **to** the woods
toward Grandmother's house!
He can even run **under** her door,
and **up** the attic stairs
with great haste
without a sound
He can run **as well as** walk
as far as Tennessee
in spite of his short legs
because of his great energy.

And so, you see, some prepositions are even made of more than one word; but the rat, ambitious little creature that he is, can still run!

PRACTICE

Exercise 1

Directions: You now have the basic information about the five parts of speech. Use the following practice to see if you understand this basic information. Determine the part of speech of the italicized word. Answers follow. When you have finished, check your answers; try to figure out *why* you went wrong—*if* you did.

1. The football fans cheered the first *down*.

2. *Down* jackets keep the wearer quite warm in very cold weather.

3. Climbing carefully *down* the ladder, he felt more and more relief as he neared the bottom.

4. The champion wrestler will *down* his opponent easily.

5. That little imp knocked *down* my carefully stacked dominoes!

6. The manager is working *outside* his realm of authority.

7. As he stepped *outside*, the wind blasted him in the face.

8. To conserve energy, we planned to insulate all the *outside* walls.

9. Those two boys really *like* baseball!

10. The Wargels painted their house green; we plan to paint ours in a *like* manner.

11. At my suggestion of a date at the movies, her face lit up *like* a neon sign.

12. I watched as my colleague *neared* the podium.

13. The burglary occurred *near* the intersection of Third and Main Streets.

14. Time draws *near!*

15. Having been involved in a *near* accident, Joyce drives more carefully now.

16. The winter's supply of firewood is *nearly* gone.

17. The horse *nearing* the finish line is being ridden by the youngest jockey here.

18. History studies the *past*.

19. His *past* actions are a good indication of what to expect in the future.

20. Thank goodness, I *passed* the course!

21. Yesterday, my sister slept *past* noon.

22. The jogger runs *past* the post office every afternoon.

Exercise 1—Answers

1. *Noun*. The clues are the article *the* and the adjective *first*. *Down* functions as a direct object of the verb *cheered*.

2. *Adjective*. It describes *what kind of* about the noun *jacket*.

3. *Preposition*. A rat can run *down the ladder*. *Down* has a noun-object: *ladder*.

4. *Verb*. *Will* is a helping verb, so its presence indicates a verb phrase.

14

5. *Adverb.* It tells *where* about *knocked*, the verb. (If you were tempted to call this one a preposition, note that the sentence can be rearranged to read, "That little imp knocked my carefully stacked dominoes down." Because *down* can be moved about in the sentence, you can guess that it functions as an adverb.)

6. *Preposition.* A rat can run *outside his realm of authority! Realm* is a noun, the object of the preposition.

7. *Adverb.* It tells *where* about the verb *stepped*.

8. *Adjective.* It tells *which ones* about the noun *walls*.

9. *Verb.* You can change the time: Yesterday, those boys really *liked* baseball.

10. *Adjective. Like* tells *what kind of* about the noun *manner*.

11. *Preposition. Like* has a noun object: *sign*. The whole phrase tells *how about lit*.

12. *Verb.* You can change the time: Tomorrow my colleague *will near* the podium.

13. *Preposition.* A rat can run *near the intersection. Intersection,* a noun, is the object of the preposition *near.* As a phrase, *near the intersection* tells *where* about the verb *occurred*.

14. *Adverb. Near* tells *where* about *draws*, the verb.

15. *Adjective. Near* tells *what kind of* about the noun *accident*.

16. *Adverb.* The *-ly* ending is a clue. So is the fact that *nearly* tells to *what extent* about *is gone*, the verb.

17. *Adjective.* Bet you goofed on that one! Did you call it a verb? *Nearing* here tells *which* about *horse:* the one *nearing the finish line*.

18. *Noun. The* is the first clue that you have a noun. *Past* also functions as the object of the verb *studies*.

19. *Adjective. Past* tells *which ones* about *actions*.

20. *Verb.* The *-ed* ending is a clue, but you need to see if that word will, in fact, change time: Tomorrow, I *will pass* the course.

21. *Preposition.* Can't a rat run *past noon?*

22. *Preposition.* Rats can run *past the post office*, too!

Exercise 2

Directions: Now try these nonsense sentences. By applying all the clues, you should be able to determine the part of speech of each of the words in these sentences! When you finish, check your answers with those below.

1. The quargle fotterstadt with yankop in its zedtop doppled lommily down the prufhoth.

2. A rewant at the moldud prampted the wobats.

3. After gundernt, an uprezeted flingle was omkled into the vifertt.

4. A langly priffert under the croddertz humphered and wekkened ikingly until edd-stodt.

5. During a dedderft in the bockfert, the okkendult's caedt is gunrothing.

Exercise 2—Answers

Sentence 1:

The—article, determines that a noun follows
quargle—adjective, modifies *fotterstadt*
fotterstadt—noun, subject
with—preposition
yankop—noun, object of the preposition *with*
in—preposition
its—adjective, modifies *zedtop*
zedtop—noun, object of the preposition *in*
doppled—verb
lommily—adverb, modifies the verb *doppled*
down—preposition
the—article, determines that a noun follows
prufhoth—noun, object of the preposition *down*

Sentence 2:

A—article, determines that a noun follows
rewant—noun, subject
at—preposition
the—article, determines that a noun follows
moldud—noun, object of preposition *at*
prampted—verb
the—article, determines that a noun follows
wobats—noun, object of the verb *prampted*

Sentence 3:

After—preposition
gundernt—noun, object of the preposition *after*
an—article, determines that a noun follows
uprezeted—adjective, modifies *flingle*
flingle—noun, subject
was omkled—verb
into—preposition
the—article, determines that a noun follows
vifertt—noun, object of the preposition *into*

Sentence 4:

A—article, determines that a noun follows
langly—adjective, modifies *priffert*
priffert—noun, subject
under—preposition
the—article, determines that a noun follows
croddertz—noun, object of the preposition *under*
humphered—verb
and—joining word
wekkened—verb
ikingly—adverb, modifies verbs *humphered* and *wekkened*
until—preposition
eddstodt—noun, object of the preposition *until*

Sentence 5:

> *During*—*preposition*
> *a*—*article,* determines that a noun follows
> *dedderft*—*noun,* object of the preposition *during*
> *in*—*preposition*
> *the*—*article,* determines that a noun follows
> *bockfert*—*noun,* object of the preposition *in*
> *the*—*article,* determines that a noun follows
> *okkendult's*—*possessive noun;* functions as adjective; modifies *caedt*
> *caedt*—*noun,* subject
> *is gunrothing*—*verb*

Exercise 3

Directions   If you were generally successful with these nonsense sentences, you will do well with the following sentences:

1. The frozen tundra offered little of interest to me.

2. Bratwurst is traditional food at the German festival.

3. Joo Ree works easily with domestic animals.

4. In the middle of the floor lay four pairs of brown shoes.

5. Ironically, eating sometimes makes me hungry!

Exercise 3—Answers

Sentence 1:

> article, adjective, noun, verb, noun (object of the verb), preposition, noun (object of the preposition), preposition, pronoun (noun substitute)

Sentence 2:

> noun, verb, adjective, noun, preposition, article, adjective, noun

Sentence 3:

> noun, verb, adverb, preposition, adjective, noun

Sentence 4:

> preposition, article, noun (object of preposition), preposition, article, noun, verb, adjective, noun (object of the verb), preposition, adjective, noun

Sentence 5:

> adverb, noun (subject of verb), adverb (modifies verb), verb, pronoun (noun substitute), adjective (modifies pronoun)

If you made reasonable progress with these sentences, you are well on your way toward mastery. Keep in mind that Chapter 2, *Parts of the Sentence*, will help you sort out and understand some specifics that may at present be unclear.

2

PARTS OF THE SENTENCE

A SENTENCE-ATTACK PLAN

Because it is important later in being able to determine correct usage, you must be able to find the major parts of the sentence:

> subject
> verb
> direct object
> indirect object
> predicate word
> objective complement

There are eight steps to a sentence-attack plan that will help you recognize the principal parts of the sentence.

Step 1: Mark out all the prepositional phrases. Remember that the prepositional phrase is the preposition *plus* the noun that is its object *plus* any words in between. (The words in between are modifiers of the object.) In other words:

> preposition
> +
> modifiers $\Bigg\}$ = prepositional phrase
> +
> noun [object]

Since prepositional phrases can function only as modifiers, they cannot function as any major part of the sentence. As a result, you will keep yourself out of trouble by eliminating them from the beginning.

> EXAMPLE: A dish of grapes was sitting on the dining room table.
> After the prepositional phrases are marked out: A dish . . . was sitting. . . .

> **NOTE:**   By eliminating *of grapes*, the prepositional phrase, you will eliminate any confusion between the nouns later when you must select the subject of the sentence.

Step 2: Find the word that changes *time*. That word will be the verb. (Be sure to find the whole verb phrase.) Remember that to make finding the verb easier, you can add the words *yesterday* or *tomorrow* in front of the sentence.

EXAMPLE: A dish of grapes was sitting on the dining-room table.

Step 1:   A dish . . . was sitting. . . .
Step 2:   A dish was sitting.
           Tomorrow, a dish *will* be sitting.
           (Helper verbs *will* and *be* are joined with the main verb, *sitting*.)
           Was sitting is the whole verb.

Step 3:   Determine whether the verb is an action verb or a linking verb. (You may need to review verb characteristics in Chapter 1, Part II, Section C.)

EXAMPLE: Some of the patients in the hall are friends of mine.

Step 1:   Some . . . are friends. . . .
Step 2:   Some are friends.
           Yesterday, some *were* friends.
           Are is the verb.
Step 3:   *Are* is a linking verb. (It is one of the verbs *to be* that are always linking.)

Step 4:   Ask *who*? or *what*? in front of the verb to determine the subject.

EXAMPLE: Most of the people at the circus reacted with surprise at the clown's antics.

Step 1:   Most . . . reacted. . . .
Step 2:   Most *reacted*.
           Tomorrow, most *will react*.
           Reacted is the verb.
Step 3:   *Reacted* is an action verb.
Step 4:   *Who* or *what* reacted?
           Answer: *most*
           Most is the subject.

Two warnings are necessary as we talk about subjects:

       Warning 1: Sometimes the subject does not appear in front of the verb. Asking *who*? or *what*? in front of the verb will still determine the subject, but you may have to look *after* the verb in the sentence in order to find the answer.

EXAMPLE: Onto the field ran the coach and his team.

Step 1:   . . . ran the coach and his team.
Step 2:   Ran the coach and his team.
           Tomorrow *will run* the coach and his team.
           Ran is the verb.
Step 3:   *Ran* is an action verb.
Step 4:   *Who* or *what* ran?
           Answer: *coach and team*.
           Coach and *team* are the subjects.

       Warning 2: The words *here* and *there* can never be subjects. (They tell *where* and usually function as adverbs.) In sentences that begin with *here* or *there*, you will have to look *after* the verb to find the subject.

EXAMPLE: There are two bowls of shelled peanuts in the cabinet.

Step 1:   There are two bowls. . . .
Step 2:   There are two bowls.
            Yesterday, there *were* two bowls.
            Are is the verb.
Step 3:   *Are* is a linking verb.
Step 4:   *Who* or *what* are?
            Answer: *bowls (Here* and *there* can never be subjects.)
            Bowls is the subject.

Step 5:   If you have a *linking* verb, skip to Step 8. If you have an *action* verb, ask *who*? or *what*? after the verb to find the direct object. (Remember, the direct object must be a noun.)

EXAMPLE: A few of the children brought their toys with them to the birthday party for my little brother.

Step 1:   A few . . . brought their toys. . . .
Step 2:   A few brought their toys.
            Tomorrow, a few *will bring* their toys.
            Brought is the verb.
Step 3:   *Brought* is an action verb.
Step 4:   *Who* or *what* brought?
            Answer: *few* (subject)
Step 5:   Since *brought* is an action verb, ask:
            Few brought *who* or *what*?
            Answer: *toys*
            Toys is the direct object.

Two warnings follow:

 Warning 1: Not all action verbs will have a direct object. Consider, for example, the sentence in the example for Step 4: *Most of the people at the circus reacted with surprise at the clown's antics.* After all the prepositional phrases were crossed out, nothing was left except *most reacted. Most* is the subject, and *reacted* is the verb. Even though *reacted* is an action verb, there is nothing to answer the questions *who*? or *what*? for the direct object. Consider this additional example:

EXAMPLE: The dark, ominous clouds moved steadily toward us from the western horizon.

Step 1:   The dark, ominous clouds moved steadily. . . .
Step 2:   The dark, ominous clouds moved steadily.
            Tomorrow, the dark, ominous clouds *will move* steadily.
            Moved is the verb.
Step 3:   *Moved* is an action verb.
Step 4:   *Who* or *what* moved?
            Answer: *clouds* (subject)
Step 5:   Since *moved* is an action verb, ask:
            Clouds moved *who* or *what*?
            Answer: none (*Steadily* tells *how*, not *who* or *what*.)
            There is no direct object.

⇨   Warning 2: There can be no direct object after a linking verb.

EXAMPLE: The water seemed deep along the bank.

Step 1:   The water seemed deep. . . .
Step 2:   The water seemed deep.
           Tomorrow, the water *will seem* deep.
           Seemed is the verb.
Step 3:   *Seemed* is a linking verb.
Step 4:   *Who* or *what* seemed?
           Answer: *water* (subject)
Step 5:   You cannot complete this step because the verb is *linking*. Go to
           Step 8.

NOTE: If you did ask the questions for the direct object (water seemed *who*
           or *what*?) you would get an answer: *deep*. But there are two prob-
           lems here:

1. You cannot have a direct object after a linking verb.
2. *Deep* is not a noun. Direct objects must be nouns.

You can see, then, why Step 3 is so important. If you neglect to determine whether the
verb is an action verb or a linking verb, you will probably get into trouble at Step 5.
   Sometimes you will find a sentence that has words that seem to answer both *who*? and
what? after the verb. Compare these two sentences:

EXAMPLE 1:   John bought ice cream and cookies.
              John bought *what*?
              Answer: *ice cream and cookies*
              (You have two direct objects joined with *and*.)
EXAMPLE 2:   John bought Sue candy.
              John bought *who* or *what*?
              Answer: *Sue and candy*?
              (It appears that *Sue* answers *who*?, and *candy* answers *what*? But
              did John buy Sue? Not quite! That leads us to Step 6.)

Step 6:   If you have a direct object, ask *to whom*? or *for whom*? to find the indirect
           object. You cannot have an indirect object if there is no direct object.

EXAMPLE: For Christmas, Barbara bought her family airline tickets to Eng-
           land.

Step 1:   . . . Barbara bought her family airline tickets. . . .
Step 2:   Barbara bought her family airline tickets.
           Tomorrow, Barbara *will buy* her family airline tickets.
           Bought is the verb.
Step 3:   *Bought* is an action verb.
Step 4:   *Who* or *what* bought?
           Answer: *Barbara* (subject)
Step 5:   Barbara bought *who* or *what*?
           Answer: *tickets* (direct object)
Step 6:   Since we have a direct object, ask:
           Barbara bought tickets *to whom* or *for whom*?
           Answer: *family*
           Family is the indirect object.

NOTE: In Step 5 you could have had two answers:

—Barbara bought *who?*
Answer: *family* (Of course, that does not really make sense. Barbara did not buy her family!)
—Barbara bought *what?*
Answer: *tickets*

Even though *family* was not a sensible answer for Step 5, if you were not thinking carefully, you could have stumbled at that point. So consider these three warnings:

 Warning 1: If there appear to be two words, one of which answers *who?* and another of which answers *what?*, the first one (which answers *who?*) is the indirect object, and the second one (which answers *what?*) is the direct object.

EXAMPLE: Laura taught her classmates a new dance step.

Step 5: Laura taught *who* or *what?*
Answer: *step* (direct object)
Step 6: Laura taught step *to whom* or *for whom?*
Answer: *classmates* (indirect object)

Classmates answers *who?* and *step* answers *what?*, so the answer to *who?* is the indirect object and the answer to *what?* is the direct object.

 Warning 2: The indirect object will always appear in the sentence between the verb and the direct object. It cannot appear after the direct object. If the sentence pattern is

noun/verb/noun/noun

then the pattern may be

subject/verb/indirect object/direct object

(See step 7 for a possible alternative pattern.)

 Warning 3: If the word *to* or *for* actually appears in front of the word you think is the indirect object, you have a prepositional phrase, not an indirect object. And you should have crossed out all prepositional phrases in Step 1!

EXAMPLE: Madelyn bought tickets for us for Saturday's concert.

Step 5: Madelyn bought *who* or *what?*
Answer: *tickets* (direct object)
Step 6: Madelyn bought tickets *to whom* or *for whom?*
Answer: none

The *for* in front of *us* makes *for us* a prepositional phrase. You can see once again the importance of Step 1. Be sure to eliminate all prepositional phrases!

Step 7: If you have a direct object and you also have a word that renames or describes the direct object, you have an objective complement instead of an indirect object. The objective complement may be either a noun or an adjective. Although we do not use this sentence structure often, we need to recognize its existence.

EXAMPLE 1:   The union elected Terry president.

Step 5:   Union elected *who* or *what*?
               Answer: *Terry* (direct object)
Step 7:   What word renames or describes *Terry*?
               Answer: *president*
               President is an objective complement.
               The noun *president* functions to rename the direct object *Terry*.

NOTE: Since *Terry* and *president* both answer the questions for the direct object, simply choose the first one for the direct object and the second one for the objective complement. The sentence pattern here is the same as for the indirect object:

noun/verb/noun/noun

But now the pattern is

subject/verb/direct object/objective complement

EXAMPLE 2:   He called me silly.

Step 5:   He called *who* or *what*?
               Answer: *me* (direct object)
Step 7:   What word renames or describes *me*?
               Answer: *silly*
               Silly is an objective complement.
               The adjective *silly* functions to describe the direct object *me*.

EXAMPLE 3:   The coach thought the play a brilliant maneuver.

Step 5:   Coach thought *who* or *what*?
               Answer: *play*
Step 7:   What word renames or describes *play*?
               Answer: *maneuver* (objective complement)

Step 8: If you have a linking verb, the word that answers *who?* or *what?* after the verb is the predicate word. The predicate word may be a noun or an adjective.

NOTE: You are asking the same questions that you did in Step 5, but now you are asking them after a *linking* verb, not an action verb.

EXAMPLE 1:   The chocolate cake on the right end of the table is especially well decorated.

Step 1:   The chocolate cake . . . is especially well decorated.
Step 2:   The chocolate cake is especially well decorated.
               Yesterday, the chocolate cake *was* especially well decorated.
               Is is the verb.
Step 3:   *Is* is the linking verb.
Step 4:   *Who* or *what is*?
               Answer: *cake* (subject)
Step 5:   If you have a linking verb, skip to Step 8.

Step 8:   Cake is *who* or *what*?
            Answer: *decorated*
            Decorated is the predicate word. It is a predicate adjective.

EXAMPLE 2: The red-haired man in the third row probably will be foreman of
            the jury.

Step 1:   The red-haired man . . . probably will be foreman. . . .
Step 2:   The red-haired man probably will be foreman.
            Yesterday, the red-haired man probably *would have been*
            foreman.
            Will be is the verb.
Step 3:   *Will be* is a linking verb.
Step 4:   *Who* or *what* will be?
            Answer: *man* (subject)
Step 5:   If you have a linking verb, skip to Step 8.
Step 8:   Man will be *who* or *what*?
            Answer: *foreman*
            Foreman is the predicate word. It is the predicate noun.

Compound Parts

Now that you have considered the eight steps of the sentence-attack plan, you need to
deal with one more concept that can apply to all eight steps:

> Any part of the sentence can be compound. The compound parts
> may be joined by the words *and, but, or,* or *nor.*

The following examples illustrate:

Step 1:   Compound object of the preposition

EXAMPLE: The sunbeams reflected through the *goblets and vases* in the jew-
            elry store's *windows and showcases.*

Step 2:   Compound verb

EXAMPLE: Shop owners *advertise* their products *and solicit* our business.

Step 3:   Compound verb, one of which is an action verb and the other of which is a
            linking verb

EXAMPLE: The track team *represented* young people from many backgrounds
            and was a melting-pot for their differences.
            (*Represented* is an action verb and *was* is a linking verb.)

Step 4:   Compound subject

EXAMPLE: *Most* of her friends *and* a few *acquaintances* showed up for the
            open-house in her honor.

Step 5:   Compound direct object

EXAMPLE: The chemist was awarded a bronze *plaque and* a $1000 cash
            prize for his work in cancer research.

Step 6:   Compound indirect object

      EXAMPLE: The guide offered *Dan or me* a free two-day fishing trip.

Step 7:   Compound objective complement

      EXAMPLE: In desperation, the mayor assigned Mr. McGilles chief *arbitrator and* mayoral *representative* in the labor dispute.

Step 8:   Compound predicate-adjective

      EXAMPLE: That cold lemonade tasted *sweet but refreshing*.

Sometimes a sentence can have several compound parts:

EXAMPLE: The grounds keeper and his assistants built the young boys and girls a long-needed bicycle path and foot trail and, as a result, are both excited and gratified by the children's positive reaction and steady use of the new facilities.

Step 1:   compound object of preposition:
reactions and *use* (also *facilities*)
Step 2:   compound verb:
built and *are*
Step 3:   compound verb, one action and the other linking:
built (action) and *are* (linking)
Step 4:   compound subject:
keeper and *assistants*
Step 5:   compound direct object:
path and *trail*
Step 6:   compound indirect object:
boys and *girls*
Step 8:   compound predicate adjectives:
excited and *gratified*

Summary for Using Commas

Step 1:   Mark out the prepositional phrases.
Step 2:   Find the verb, the word that changes time.
Step 3:   Determine whether the verb is an action verb or a linking verb.
Step 4:   Ask *who?* or *what?* in front of the verb to determine the subject. (*Who* or *what* [verb]?)
Step 5:   If you have a linking verb, skip to Step 8. If you have an action verb, ask *who?* or *what?* after the verb to find the direct object. ([Subject][verb] *who or what?*)
Step 6:   If you have a direct object, ask *to whom?* or *for whom?* after the direct object to find the indirect object.
Step 7:   Any word that renames or describes the direct object is the objective complement.
Step 8:   If you have a linking verb, ask *who?* or *what?* after the verb to find the predicate word.

PRACTICE

Exercise 1

Directions: For practice, consider the following questions about the general ideas in the sentence-attack plan. Check your answers with those at the end of these questions. No cheating, now!

1. Can you have a compound subject?

2. Can you have a direct object after a linking verb?

3. Must you have an indirect object after a direct object?

4. Do action verbs take predicate words?

5. Will most linking verbs have predicate words?

6. Will all action verbs have direct objects?

7. Can you have an indirect object without a direct object?

8. Can a sentence have both a predicate word and a direct object?

9. Can the verb be more than one word?

10. Can there be more than one verb in a sentence?

11. Can there be both a linking verb and an action verb in the same sentence?

12. Can direct objects appear after action verbs?

13. Can there be two direct objects in a sentence?

14. Can a sentence have both a direct object and an objective complement?

15. Can a sentence have both a direct object and an indirect object?

16. Must a sentence have a subject?

17. Will the subject appear in front of the verb?

18. Will all sentences have a verb?

19. Will all sentences have either a direct object or a predicate word?

20. Are all subjects, direct objects, indirect objects, predicate words, and objective complements nouns?

Exercise 1—Answers

1. *Yes. Example:* My *sister* and *Georgette* are going shopping.

2. *No.* Direct objects must follow action verbs.

3. *No.* A direct object may exist without an indirect object.

4. *No.* Predicate words follow linking verbs.

5. *Yes.* Most linking verbs will have a predicate word, but sometimes that predicate word is implied. *Example:* Is Sue your sister? Yes, she is. (*My sister* are the implied predicate words.)

6. *No. Example:* Joanne jogs after work every day. Joanne jogs *who* or *what*? Answer: none.

7. *No.* There must be a direct object before there can be an indirect object.

8. *Yes,* but only if there are *both* an action verb and a linking verb.

9. *Yes.* The verb often has helpers.

10. *Yes. Example:* Barbara *bought* and *delivered* the flowers herself.

11. *Yes. Example:* The young athlete *ran* seven miles and *was* exhausted.

12. *Yes.* Not every action verb, however, must have a direct object.

13. *Yes. Example:* Our members read both newspaper *reports* and magazine *articles* about the dispute.

14. *Yes.* The objective complement renames or describes the direct object, so there must be a direct object before there can be an objective complement.

15. *Yes.* A sentence must have a direct object before it can have an indirect object, but the direct object may exist without an indirect object.

16. *Yes,* of course!

17. *Not always.* Remember that *here* and *there*, for instance, cannot be subjects; the subject will have to come after the verb in that case. There are other situations, too, of course, in which the subject comes later.

18. *Yes!*

19. *No.* Since an action verb may exist without a direct object and since, in some cases, linking verbs have only implied predicate words, a sentence may exist—and often does, in fact—with only a subject and a verb.

20. *No.* Predicate words and objective complements may be nouns or adjectives.

Exercise 2

Directions: Now that you have practiced the sentence-attack plan, try applying the eight steps to the following sentences. You will need to apply, also, the information you learned in Chapter 1. Label the following items in these sentences:

subject
verb
direct object, if any
indirect object, if any
objective complement, if any
predicate word, if any

When you finish, check your answers on the following pages.

1. The professor, with some help from his niece, found his car keys behind the cushion.

2. A couple of my friends seemed especially pleased with their respective successes at the track meet.

3. One of the cheerleaders fell during the half-time show and twisted his left ankle.

4. The mayor sent the City Council her ideas for improving city traffic flow.

5. We bought three back issues of *National Geographic* for your use.

6. Do you really understand these solutions to the problem?

7. The essay-contest winners were a boy in my neighborhood and a girl in the next town.

8. Funds from the state government made local road improvements possible.

9. With his courage, he will win a medal for bravery.

10. Most young speakers appear nervous but usually steel themselves with determination.

11. The basketball referee called the player's action a personal foul.

12. Some of these civic-minded people have been buying their out-of-town friends souvenirs from our city.

Exercise 2—Answers

Sentence 1: The professor, with some help from his niece, found his car keys behind the cushion.

    Step 1: The professor . . . found his car keys. . . .
    Step 2: The professor found his car keys.
           Tomorrow, the professor *will find* his car keys.
           Found is the verb.
    Step 3: *Found* is an action verb.
    Step 4: *Who* or *what* found?
           Answer: *professor* (subject)
    Step 5: Professor found *who* or *what?*
           Answer: *keys* (direct object)
    Step 6: Professor found keys to *whom* or *for whom?*
           Answer: none

Sentence 2: A couple of my friends seemed especially pleased with their respective successes at the track meet.

    Step 1: A couple . . . seemed especially pleased. . . .
    Step 2: A couple seemed especially pleased.
           Tomorrow, a couple *will seem* especially pleased.
           Seemed is the verb.
    Step 3: *Seemed* is a linking verb.
    Step 4: *Who* or *what* seemed?
           Answer: *couple* (subject)
    Step 5: If you have a linking verb, skip to Step 8.
    Step 8: Couple seemed *who* or *what?*
           Answer: *pleased* (predicate word)

Sentence 3: One of the cheerleaders fell during the half-time show and twisted his left ankle.

    Step 1: One . . . fell . . . and twisted his left ankle.
    Step 2: One fell and twisted his left ankle.
           Tomorrow, one *will fall* and *twist* his left ankle.
           Fell and *twisted* are the verbs.
    Step 3: *Fell* and *twisted* are both action verbs.
    Step 4: *Who* or *what* fell and twisted?
           Answer: *one* (subject)
    Step 5: One fell *who* or *what?*
           Answer: none

One twisted *who* or *what?*
Answer: *ankle* (direct object)
Step 6: One twisted ankle *to whom* or *for whom?*
Answer: none

Sentence 4: The mayor sent the City Council her ideas for improving city traffic flow.

Step 1: The mayor sent the City Council her ideas. . . .
Step 2: The mayor sent the City Council her ideas.
Tomorrow, the mayor *will send* the City Council her ideas.
Sent is the verb.
Step 3: *Sent* is an action verb.
Step 4: *Who* or *what* sent?
Answer: *mayor* (subject)
Step 5: Mayor sent *who* or *what?*
Answer: *ideas* (direct object)
Step 6: Mayor sent ideas *to whom* or *for whom?*
Answer: *City Council* (indirect object)

Sentence 5: We bought three back issues of *National Geographic* for your use.

Step 1: We bought three back issues. . . .
Step 2: We bought three back issues.
Tomorrow, we *will buy* three back issues.
Bought is the verb.
Step 3: *Bought* is an action verb.
Step 4: *Who* or *what* bought?
Answer: *we* (subject)
Step 5: We bought *who* or *what?*
Answer: *issues* (direct object)
Step 6: We bought issues *to whom* or *for whom?*
Answer: none (Remember, *for your use* is a prepositional phrase.)

Sentence 6: Do you really understand these solutions to the problem?

Step 1: Do you really understand these solutions. . . .
Step 2: Do you really understand these solutions?
Yesterday, *did* you really *understand* these solutions?
Do understand is the verb.
(Did you remember that *do* is usually a helping verb?)
Step 3: *Do understand* is an action verb.
Step 4: *Who* or *what* do understand?
Answer: *you* (subject)
Step 5: You do understand *who* or *what?*
Answer: *solutions* (direct object)
Step 6: You do understand solutions *to whom* or *for whom?*
Answer: none
(You didn't answer with *problems,* did you? Remember, you crossed that out
in the prepositional phrase in Step 1.)

Sentence 7: The essay-contest winners were a boy in my neighborhood and a girl in the
next town.

Step 1: The essay-contest winners were a boy . . . and a girl. . . .
Step 2: The essay-contest winners were a boy and a girl.
Tomorrow, the essay-contest winners *will be* a boy and a girl.
Were is the verb.

Step 3: *Were* is a linking verb.
Step 4: *Who* or *what* were?
  Answer: *winners* (subject)
Step 5: If you have a linking verb, skip to Step 8.
Step 8: Winners were *who* or *what*?
  Answer: *boy and girl* (compound predicate words)

Sentence 8: Funds from the state government made local road improvements possible.

Step 1: Funds . . . made local road improvements possible.
Step 2: Funds made local road improvements possible.
  Tomorrow, funds *will make* local road improvements possible.
  Made is the verb.
Step 3: *Made* is an action verb.
Step 4: *Who* or *what* made?
  Answer: *funds* (subject)
Step 5: Funds made *who* or *what*?
  Answer: *improvements* (direct object)
Step 6: Funds made improvements *to whom* or *for whom*?
  Answer: none
Step 7: What word renames or describes the direct object?
  Answer: *possible* (objective complement)

Sentence 9: With his courage, he will win a medal for bravery.

Step 1: . . . he will win a medal. . . .
Step 2: He will win a medal.
  Yesterday, he *won* a medal.
  Will win is the verb.
Step 3: *Will win* is an action verb.
Step 4: *Who* or *what* will win?
  Answer: *he* (subject)
Step 5: He will win *who* or *what*?
  Answer: *medal* (direct object)
Step 6: He will win medal *to whom* or *for whom*?
  Answer: none

Sentence 10: Most young speakers appear nervous but usually steel themselves with determination.

Step 1: Most young speakers appear nervous but usually steel themselves. . . .
Step 2: Most young speakers appear nervous but usually steel themselves.
  Tomorrow, most young speakers *will appear* nervous but usually *will steel* themselves.
  Appear and *steel* are the verbs.
Step 3: *Appear* is a linking verb. (Substitute *are* to test the verb.)
  Steel is an action verb.
Step 4: *Who* or *what* appear?
  Answer: *speakers* (subject)
  Who or *what* steel?
  Answer: *speakers* (subject)
Step 5: (Here is the tricky part. You have *both* an action verb and a linking verb. So you will need to do Step 5 with the verb *steel* and skip to Step 8 with the verb *appear*.)
  Speakers steel *who* or *what*?
  Answer: *themselves* (direct object)

Step 6: Speakers steel themselves *to whom* or *for whom*?
    Answer: none
Step 8: Speakers appear *who* or *what*?
    Answer: *nervous* (predicate word)

Sentence 11: The basketball referee called the player's action a personal foul.

Step 1: The basketball referee called the player's action a personal foul. (no prepositional phrases)
Step 2: The basketball referee called the player's action a personal foul.
    Tomorrow, the basketball referee *will call* the player's action a personal foul.
    Called is the verb.
Step 3: *Called* is an action verb.
Step 4: *Who* or *what called?*
    Answer: referee (subject)
Step 5: Referee called *who* or *what*?
    Answer: *action* (direct object)
    (Since there appear to be two answers to the question, we know that we need to go on to Step 7.)
Step 7: What word renames or describes the direct object?
    Answer: *foul* (objective complement)

Sentence 12: Some of these civic-minded people have been buying their out-of-town friends souvenirs from our city.

Step 1: Some . . . have been buying their out-of-town friends souvenirs. . . .
Step 2: Some have been buying their out-of-town friends souvenirs.
    Yesterday, some *had been buying* their out-of-town friends souvenirs.
    Have been buying is the verb.
Step 3: *Have been buying* is an action verb.
Step 4: *Who* or *what* have been buying?
    Answer: *some* (subject)
Step 5: Some have been buying *who* or *what*?
    Answer: *souvenirs* (direct object)
    (Remember, they did not buy their friends!)
Step 6: Some have been buying souvenirs *to whom* or *for whom*?
    Answer: *friends* (indirect object)

II
USAGE

3

AGREEMENT OF SUBJECT AND VERB

Now that you have grasped the basics of general "grammar," we are ready to talk about the real problems with writing and speaking: usage.

Agreement of subject and verb is, for the most part, a natural speech pattern. Most of us grew up learning to say "The boy walks" and "The boys walk." We would never say "The boy walk" or "They walks." Sometimes, however, problem situations occur in which our "natural" patterns defeat us. These situations are what we need to talk about in this chapter.

BASIC PREMISES

Let us start with three basic premises:

1. Subjects can be singular or plural.

> EXAMPLES: The *apple* (singular) is rotten.
> The *apples* (plural) are rotten.

2. Verbs can be singular or plural.

> EXAMPLES: The child *talks* (singular) constantly.
> The children *talk* (plural) constantly.

> **NOTE:** Subjects add -s to form the *plural*, and verbs add -s to form the *singular*. *Apple* is singular. *Talks* is singular. *Apples* is plural. *Talk* is plural.

3. Subjects must agree in number with their verbs. Singular subjects must have singular verbs. Plural subjects must have plural verbs.

> EXAMPLES: *He* (singular subject) *walks* (singular verb).
> *They* (plural subject) *walk* (plural verb).

With these basic premises in mind, let us now consider the problems that occur in subject-verb agreement:

PROBLEMS

Problem 1: A problem occurs when the writer is confused about choosing the subject. Since the verb must agree with its subject, not recognizing the subject will result in a glaring error! (A review of Chapter 2 may help here.) Three specific situations seem to cause the greatest problems:

Situation A: Sometimes the writer has difficulty locating the subject when words come between the subject and its verb. These words may be prepositional phrases, verbal phrases, or clauses. Such words cause a problem because the writer's "natural" patterns make him want the verb to agree with the nearest noun—which may not be the subject.

> EXAMPLE 1: The box of apples is beginning to rot.
> (*Is beginning* must agree with its subject *box*, not with *apples* in the prepositional phrase.)
>
> EXAMPLE 2: The cars, washed and shined with care, sit ready for the parade.
> (*Sit* must agree with its subject *cars*. The verbal phrase *washed and shined with care* cannot alter the subject-verb agreement.)
>
> EXAMPLE 3: Those motorcycles that roar up and down the street cause disturbance for the hospital.
> (*Cause* must agree with its subject, *motorcycles*. The clause *that roar up and down the street* cannot alter the subject-verb agreement.)

⇨ Warning: Some prepositional phrases logically make a subject appear to be plural:

with	as well as
along with	in addition to
together with	

But prepositional phrases *cannot* alter the noun-subject.

> EXAMPLE 1: The doctor, together with his two assistants, is working desperately.
> (*Is working* must agree with its subject, *doctor*. The prepositional phrase *together with his two assistants* cannot alter the subject-verb agreement, even though logic wants you to call that verb plural.)
>
> EXAMPLE 2: My neighbor, along with her two German shepherds, walks across the pasture daily to visit.
> (*Walks* must agree with its subject, *neighbor*. Do not let the prepositional phrase *along with her two German shepherds* interfere.)
>
> EXAMPLE 3: The television set, in addition to the hot water heater and the furnace, was damaged by the lightning.
> (*Was* agrees with the subject *set*. Ignore those prepositional phrases!)

Situation B: Sometimes the writer may have difficulty locating the subject when the subject comes after the verb. If, for instance, the sentence begins with *here* or *there*, the subject comes *after* the verb.

EXAMPLE 1: There are three seats empty.
(Seats *are*.)
EXAMPLE 2: Here is the letter I was looking for.
(Letter *is*).

Other sentences may also have the subject appearing after the verb:

EXAMPLE 1: Into the office charge the supervisor and her assistant.
(Supervisor and assistant *charge*.)
EXAMPLE 2: Where are the old newspapers?
(Newspapers *are*.)
EXAMPLE 3: Who are the girl in the ski outfit and the girl in the tennis dress?
(Girl and girl *are*.)

Situation C: Sometimes the writer is confused by the choice of subject if the subject is singular and the predicate word is plural—or vice-versa. He may think the verb *sounds* wrong; but the verb must agree with its subject, not its predicate word.

EXAMPLE 1: Physical conditioning and mental attitude are the winning combination.
(Conditioning and attitude *are*.)
EXAMPLE 2: The winning combination is physical conditioning and mental attitude.
(Combination *is*.)

Problem 2: A problem occurs when indefinite pronouns appear. There are three groups of indefinite pronouns:

Group A: Indefinite pronouns that are always singular:

someone	anyone	everyone
somebody	anybody	everybody
each	one	either
nobody	no one	neither

The easiest way to remember these singular words is to think *single* one or one with *each*:

some [single] *one*
some [single] *body*
every [single] *one*
each [single one]
neither [one]

EXAMPLE 1: *Everyone* in the offices is too warm to work effectively.
(Think, "every [single] one *is*.")
EXAMPLE 2: *Neither* of the mechanics wants to work on Sunday.
(Think, "neither [one] *wants*.")
EXAMPLE 3: *Everybody* seated in the last two rows resents being asked to move forward.
(Think, "every [single] body *resents*.")

EXAMPLE 4:   *Each* of my friends calls me once a week.
(Think, "each [one] *calls*.")

Group B: Indefinite pronouns that are always plural:

several
few
both
many

These words are especially easy to remember since they all *mean* "more than one."

EXAMPLE 1:   Both of the books require careful reading.
(Both *require*.)
EXAMPLE 2:   Several of the fielders regularly run four or five miles a day.
(Several *run*.)

Group C: Indefinite pronouns that can be singular or plural:

some	all
any	most
none	

To determine whether these words are singular or plural, look at the prepositional phrase that follows.

EXAMPLE 1:   Some of the sugar is on the floor.
(Since *some* can be singular or plural, look at *sugar* to decide: *sugar is*.)
EXAMPLE 2:   Some of the apples are in the sink.
(Since *some* can be singular or plural, look at *apples* to decide: *apples are*.)

Problem 3:   A problem occurs when there are compound subjects. Three kinds of compound situations occur:

Situation A: Two subjects joined by *and* will always take a plural verb:

1 and 1	=	2
doctor and nurse		work
1 and 2	=	3
doctor and nurses		work
2 and 1	=	3
doctors and nurse		work

NOTE: Some peculiar combinations occur that are logically singular. For these, use the singular verb.

EXAMPLE 1:   *Peaches and cream is* my favorite desert.
EXAMPLE 2:   *My sister and best friend is* Mary Ann.

Situation B: Two singular subjects joined by *or* or *nor* will take a singular verb:

1 or 1	=	1
doctor or nurse		*works*
1 nor 1	=	0
doctor nor nurse		*works*

Situation C: A singular subject and a plural subject joined by *or* or *nor* will take a singular or plural verb, depending on which subject is nearer the verb:

1	or	2	=	2
doctor	or	*nurses work*		
2	or	1	=	1
doctors	or	*nurse works*		
1	nor	2	=	2
doctor	nor	*nurses work*		
2	nor	1	=	1
doctors	nor	*nurse works*		

Consider the following examples for all three compound-subject situations:

EXAMPLE 1: Neither Ellen *nor* her *cousins are* planning a vacation.
(1 nor 2 = 2)
EXAMPLE 2: Neither her cousins *nor Ellen is* planning a vacation.
(2 nor 1 = 1)
EXAMPLE 3: Both her cousins *and Ellen are* planning a vacation.
(2 and 1 = 3)
EXAMPLE 4: Ellen *or* her *cousin is* planning a vacation.
(1 or 1 = 1)

Problem 4: A problem occurs when the subject is a collective noun that can be singular or plural. Collective nouns are nouns that represent a group: *team, jury, cast, class, crew, audience.*

Situation A: Collective nouns are *singular* when the group works together as a unit.

EXAMPLE 1: The *team runs* enthusiastically onto the floor.
(The team works together as a unit.)
EXAMPLE 2: The *jury has reached* its verdict.
(The jury functions as a unit in reaching a verdict.)

Situation B: Collective nouns are *plural* when the members of the group are acting individually.

EXAMPLE 1: The *team are putting* on their uniforms.
(Each team member acts individually to put on his own uniform. If we said, "The team *is* putting on its uniform," we would have the entire team in one uniform! How unhandy!)
EXAMPLE 2: The *jury have argued* for three hours.
(Each individual jury member is presenting his point of view.)

☞ Hint: Often the meaning of the sentence will tell you whether the collective noun is singular or plural, but sometimes additional hints appear—like plural pronouns.

EXAMPLE 1: The jury reaches *its* decision after much deliberation.
(The singular *its* gave a hint that *jury* is singular.)

EXAMPLE 2: The crew take *their places* five minutes before curtain time.
(The plural *their* and *places* give a hint that *crew* is plural. Of course, the entire crew could not be in one spot anyway!)

Problem 5: A problem occurs when words look plural but are not. Three such situations occur.

Situation A: Some words end in *-s* but represent a single thing: *news, measles, mumps*. These words need singular verbs.

EXAMPLE 1: The six o'clock *news is* about to begin.
EXAMPLE 2: *Measles* sometimes *has* rather serious side effects.

 Warning: Some words end in *-s* and *seem* to represent a single thing, but there are two *parts* to that single thing. Then the verb is plural. Consider words like *pants, scissors, trousers, shears,* and *pliers*.

EXAMPLE 1: The *scissors are* on the desk.
EXAMPLE 2: Here *are* the *pliers*.

Situation B: Words that end in *-ics* are usually singular: *politics, mathematics, civics, ethics, economics, athletics*. These words are *singular* when they refer to a study, science, or practice.

EXAMPLE 1: *Politics is* an interesting avocation.
EXAMPLE 2: *Mathematics is* his favorite subject.
EXAMPLE 3: *Economics is* a course required for high school graduation.

 Warning: These words are *plural* when they have modifiers in front of them.

EXAMPLE 1: *His politics are* somewhat divided.
(The singular modifier *his* makes *politics* plural.)
EXAMPLE 2: *The mathematics* of the tax return *are* flawless.
(*The* makes *mathematics* plural.)
EXAMPLE 3: *The school's athletics are* all for both males and females.
(The modifiers *the school's* make *athletics* plural.)

Situation C: Some words that have become part of our language retain their original foreign plural forms:

Singular	Plural
datum	data
alumnus	alumni
memorandum	memoranda

Because we usually see these words in the plural form, we sometimes forget the singular form and thereby use the wrong verb form. Consider these examples:

EXAMPLE 1:   The *data were collected* by a licensed agency.

EXAMPLE 2:   The *memoranda are* easily *read and understood*.

Situation D: Titles that are plural still represent a single thing, so the title needs a singular verb.

EXAMPLE 1:   <u>Great Expectations</u> *presents* universal themes for all of us to consider.

EXAMPLE 2:   <u>A Man for All Seasons</u> *is playing* at our local theater.

Situation E: Some nouns in the plural form represent an amount, a fraction, or an element of time. Those nouns are considered *singular*.

☞   Hint: Try substituting the words *that amount* for the phrase. If the substitution works, the phrase is singular. If you need to substitute with *that number,* for countable items, then the phrase is plural.

EXAMPLE 1:   *Sixty minutes is* too much time to spend eating.
(*That amount* of time is too much time to spend eating.)

Compare: *Sixty minutes seem* to be passing rapidly on the timer's clock!
(*That number* of minutes—countable—is passing.)

EXAMPLE 2:   *Five dollars is* what that hamburger costs.
(*That amount* is what that hamburger costs.)

Compare: *Five one-dollar bills are* all he had with him.
(*That number* of bills—countable—is what he had.)

EXAMPLE 3:   *Three-fourths* of the pie *is* gone.
(*That amount* of the pie is gone.)

Compare: *Three-fourths* of the cars *are* gone from the parking lot.
(*That number* is gone. Cars are countable.)

EXAMPLE 4:   *Sixty pounds is* an excessive weight to mail.
(*That amount* is an excessive weight.)

Compare: *Sixty pounds* of cornmeal *were* sold to sixty customers yesterday. (*That number* of pounds were sold.)

If you can master these five problems, chances are you will have little or no difficulty in using the correct verb form to agree with the subject.

PRACTICE

Exercise 1

Directions: Try the following sentences to test yourself for understanding of all ten rules. Check your answers with those that follow. Problem and situation references are given so that you can review anything you may not yet have mastered.

1. An Indian headdress and two beaded moccasins (was/were) in the museum window.

2. The boss's memoranda (is/are) filed away safely.

3. The neighbor, along with three of his friends, (is/are) going to Canada for a fishing trip.

4. Few of the trees (lose/loses) their leaves in spring.

5. *Three Faces of Eve* (is/are) a study in psychology.

6. Someone in one of these neighborhoods (is/are) on the mayor's investigative committee.

7. His ethics (requires/require) scrutiny.

8. All his friends (wishes/wish) him well and hope that all happiness (is/are) his.

9. None of the sunshine (seeps/seep) into the inner part of the house.

10. Everybody (knows/know) his part!

11. We thought five dollars (was/were) a fair donation.

12. Neither of the young men (was/were) recognized for outstanding contributions.

13. Neither the managers nor the supervisor (understands/understand) the complexity of the situation.

14. The crew (was/were) working at their respective jobs.

15. The bowl of bananas (is/are) tempting.

16. Everyone in the room (sees/see) opportunity knocking.

17. The baby and his mother (is/are), according to all reports, doing well.

18. Any of the nails that you don't use (is/are) returnable.

19. Although it is usually thought of as a childhood disease, measles (is/are) even more serious as an adult disease.

20. Mathematics (is/are) his favorite subject.

21. I hope somebody (sings/sing) the national anthem.

22. His hobby (is/are) butterflies.

23. Neither the carpenter nor the cabinet maker (was/were) willing to build the fancy shelves.

24. Both (is/are) excellent lecturers.

25. The city's economics (is/are) unsettled.

26. The financial advisor, in addition to the City Council members, (plans/plan) to complete additional reports for the year's end.

42

27. Their team usually (has/have) a successful season.

28. Miss Altheide or her two nieces (plans/plan) to attend the card party.

29. Some students (is/are) hoping that some achievement (is/are) forthcoming.

30. His tractor, as well as the plows, discs, and drills, (needs/need) regular maintenance.

31. Oil lamps (is/are) a good source of light.

32. Either crickets or minnows (makes/make) good fishing bait.

33. Three-fourths of his chickens (is/are) good layers.

34. Onto the rodeo grounds (charges/charge) a wild bull.

35. Politics (enters/enter) nearly everyone's life.

36. Seven one-dollar bills (brings/bring) him luck, he thinks.

37. Two cats and a dog (sleeps/sleep) together at my house.

38. That tree, which has heart-shaped leaves, (is/are) especially ornamental.

39. *Sixty Minutes* usually (airs/air) on Sunday evening.

40. Neither the roll-top desk nor the two electric typewriters (belongs/belong) to him.

41. As soon as the data (is/are) collected, the administration can give the results.

42. Athletics (is/are) a major part of her life.

43. The cast (performs/perform) admirably.

44. Either the scrubber or the precipitator (is/are) not functioning properly at the power-generating plant.

45. There (is/are) three people waiting to talk with the congressman.

Exercise 1—Answers

1. headress and moccasins *were* (Problem 3, Situation A)

2. memoranda *are* (Problem 5, Situation C)

3. neighbor *is* (Problem 1, Situation A)

4. few *lose* (Problem 2, Group B)

5. *Three Faces of Eve is* (Problem 5, Situation D)

6. someone *is* (Problem 2, Group A)

7. ethics *require* (Problem 5, Situation B)

8. all (friends) *wish and hope* (Problem 2, Group C) all (happiness) *is* (Problem 2, Group C)

9. none (sunshine) *seeps* (Problem 2, Group C)

10. everybody *knows* (Problem 2, Group A)

11. five dollars (that amount) *was* (Problem 5, Situation E)

12. neither *was* (Problem 2, Group A)

13. neither managers nor supervisor *understands* (Problem 3, Situation C)

14. crew *were* at *their* jobs (Problem 4, Situation B)

15. bowl *is* (Problem 1, Situation A)

16. everyone *sees* (Problem 2, Group A)

17. baby and mother *are* (Problem 3, Situation A)

18. any (nails) *are* (Problem 2, Group C)

19. measles *is* (Problem 5, Situation A)

20. mathematics *is* (Problem 5, Situation B)

21. somebody *sings* (Problem 2, Group A)

22. hobby *is* (Problem 1, Situation C)

23. neither carpenter nor cabinet maker *was* (Problem 3, Situation B)

24. both *are* (Problem 2, Group B)

25. economics *are* (Problem 5, Situation B)

26. advisor *plans* (Problem 1, Situation A)

27. team *has* (Problem 4, Situation A)

28. Miss Altheide or nieces *plan* (Problem 3, Situation C)

29. some (students) *are* (Problem 2, Group C) some (achievement) *is* (Problem 2, Group C)

30. tractor *needs* (Problem 1, Situation A)

31. lamps *are* (Problem 1, Situation C)

32. either crickets or minnows *make* (Problem 2, Group A)

33. three-fourths (that number of chickens) *are* (Problem 5, Situation E)

34. bull *charges* (Problem 1, Situation B)

35. politics *enters* (Problem 5, Situation B)

36. bills (that number) *bring* (Problem 5, Situation E)

37. cats and a dog *sleep* (Problem 3, Situation A)

38. tree *is* (Problem 1, Situation A)

39. *Sixty Minutes airs* (Problem 5, Situation D)

40. neither desk nor typewriters *belong* (Problem 3, Situation C)

41. data *are* (Problem 5, Situation C)

42. athletics *is* (Problem 5, Situation B)

43. cast *performs* (Problem 4, Situation A)

44. either scrubber or precipitator *is* (Problem 3, Situation B)

45. people *are* (Problem 1, Situation B)

Exercise 2

Directions: Now that you have worked your way through isolated sentences, apply your understanding to the following passage. Correct any subject-verb agreement errors you spot, and then check your answers below.

(1) When the artists and Ms. Karl comes to Lewisport to exhibit their work, spectators will see a wide variety of styles and media. (2) For instance, the paintings from the student group shows works in oil and tempera. (3) Pastels or ink drawings show representative works by the master herself. (4) Because the media Ms. Karl uses is widely varied, her most successful students' work shows a blend of techniques, all learned from Karl's examples. (5) Neither the students nor Ms. Karl, however, is recognized for work in sculpture, and works in any kind of wood tends to be primitive at best. (6) Nevertheless, a visitor to the exhibit, like the art critics themselves, is likely to find something impressive. (7) Since ethics are not part of the exhibit, however, some critics may find certain artistic subject matter to be in poor taste.

Exercise 2—Answers

Sentence 1:

artists and Ms. Karl *come* (Problem 3, Situation A)

Sentence 2:

paintings *show* (Problem 1, Situation A)

Sentence 3:

(correct)

Sentence 4:

media *are* (Problem 5, Situation C)

Sentence 5:

works *tend* (Problem 1, Situation A)

Sentence 6:

(correct)

Sentence 7:

ethics *is* (Problem 5, Situation B)

4

PRONOUN USAGE

Pronouns, earlier called simply noun substitutes, can be a source of frustration only because a writer may not be sure which pronoun to use. Should he say "between you and I" or "between you and me"? Should he say "Us voters are registered" or "We voters are registered"? Should he say "Among those who called are George, Bill, and me" or ". . . George, Bill, and I"?

Ten easy rules should solve all these problems.

RULES

RULE 1: The pronoun-subject of a sentence must be one of these pronouns:

I, you, he, she, it, we, or *they*

☞ Hint: Usually a writer has no difficulty with this rule unless confused by compound parts.

EXAMPLE: Barbara and (he/him) went to the new shopping mall.

To Test: Use the pronoun alone. Cross out the plural parts:
. . . *he* went to the new shopping mall.

EXAMPLE: My sister and (her/she) planned to watch the late show.
. . . *she* planned to watch the late show.

RULE 2: If the pronoun is a predicate word, it must be in the same form as the subject. In other words, after a linking verb, you must use one of the following pronouns:

I, you, he, she, it, we, or *they*

EXAMPLES: It *was I* who called last night.
(I was.)

The man you need to see *is he* in the other room.
(He is.)

The people whom we met *were George and he.*
(George and he were.)

46

RULE 3: If a pronoun is an object (direct object, indirect object, object of a preposition), use one of these pronouns:

me, you, him, her, it, us, or *them*

☞ Hint 1: If you have trouble remembering which pronouns are used as objects, say the pronoun with *to*:

to me, to you, to him, to us, to them

☞ Hint 2: As in Rule 1, you will probably have no trouble until you meet compound parts.

To Test: Cross out the compound parts.

EXAMPLE 1: The newspaper named Jose and (he/him) as the award recipients.
The newspaper named . . . *him* as the award recipients.
(*Him* is a direct object.)

EXAMPLE 2: The carnival man sold (I/me) and (she/her) three tickets.
The carnival man sold *me* . . . three tickets.
(*Me* is an indirect object.)
The carnival man sold . . . *her* three tickets.
(*Her* is an indirect object.)

EXAMPLE 3: The Bumbler of the Year Award was given to (he/him) and (I/me).
The Bumbler of the Year Award was given to *him* . . .
(*Him* is an object of the preposition *to*.)
The Bumbler of the Year Award was given to . . . *me*.
(*Me* is an object of the preposition *to*.)

RULE 4: When a noun immediately follows a pronoun, cross out the noun to make finding the correct pronoun easier.

EXAMPLE 1: (We/Us) beekeepers are a rather small group.
We . . . are a rather small group.

EXAMPLE 2: The policeman helped (we/us) motorists through the heavily traveled intersection.
The policeman helped *us* . . . through the heavily traveled intersection.

EXAMPLE 3: It was (we/us) taxpayers who needed help.
It was *we* . . . who needed help.
(Remember the linking verb here! That is Rule 2.)

RULE 5: When there is a pronoun in a comparison, complete the comparison to help you find the correct pronoun. (You can complete the comparison by adding a verb.)

EXAMPLE 1: He is taller than (I/me).
He is taller than *I* [am].

EXAMPLE 2:   Jeremy works harder than (he/him).
Jeremy works harder than *he* [does].

EXAMPLE 3:   This young lady is as clever as (he/him).
This young lady is as clever as *he* [is].

RULE 6:   Use a possessive pronoun with *-ing* nouns.

EXAMPLE 1:   We were offended by *his singing.*
We were not offended by him, only by his singing.

EXAMPLE 2:   Earl objected to *my getting* home late.
(Earl did not object to me. He objected to my getting home late. *My* becomes an adjective modifying *getting*.)

EXAMPLE 3:   *His talking* caused him constant problems.
(*His* is an adjective modifying *talking*. Possessive pronouns are the only pronouns that can function as adjectives.)

EXAMPLE 4:   *Our* frequent *walking* gives me blisters.
(*Our* is an adjective modifying *walking*. It must be a possessive pronoun.)

RULE 7:   When a pronoun is used as an appositive, it is in the same form as the word to which it refers. An appositive is a noun that renames another noun preceding it and is set off with commas: *My boss, Mr. Ratherwood, collects Indian relics. Mr. Ratherwood,* the appositive, renames *boss*. If the appositive refers to a subject, you will use the subject form. If the appositive refers to an object, you will use the object form. If the appositive refers to a predicate word, use the subject form.

EXAMPLE 1:   The two elected to the County Council, Gerry and (he/him), spoke to us.
Gerry and (he/him) is the appositive and refers to the subject, *two*. Since the appositive refers to a subject, you will use the subject form, *he*.

EXAMPLE 2:   The chairman introduced the evening's two speakers, Dorothea and (I/me).
Dorothea and (I/me) is the appositive and refers to the object *speakers*. Since the appositive refers to an object, you will use the object form, *me*.

☞   Hint: To make the decision easier, try these two steps:
Step 1:   Cross out the word or words to which the appositive refers.
Step 2:   Read without any compound parts.

Application 1:
Step 1:   The two elected to the County Council, Gerry and (he/him), spoke to us.
. . . Gerry and (he/him), spoke to us.
Step 2:   . . . (he/him) spoke to us.
Solution: *He* spoke to us.

Application 2:

Step 1:	Martin worked at the sawmill with his two friends, Billy Joe and (he/him).
	Martin worked at the sawmill with . . . Billy Joe and (he/him).
Step 2:	Martin worked at the sawmill with . . . (he/him).
Solution:	Martin worked at the sawmill with *him*.

Application 3:

Step 1:	Two neighbors were professional photographers, Mrs. Martin and (he/him).
	Two neighbors were . . . Mrs. Martin and (he/him).
Step 2:	Two neighbors were . . . (he/him).
Solution:	Two neighbors were *he* (and Mrs. Martin). (Remember to use the subject form after the linking verb! That is Rule 2 again!)

RULE 8: Do not use a compound pronoun unless the word it refers to is in the same sentence. The following are compound pronouns:

myself	herself	yourselves
yourself	itself	themselves
himself	ourselves	

EXAMPLE 1: Incorrect: Those who bid on the barnwood picture frames were Mr. Lewis, Miss Qualls, and myself.
Correct: Those who bid on the barnwood picture frames were Mr. Lewis, Miss Qualls, and *I*.

EXAMPLE 2: Incorrect: Himself was selected leader.
Correct: He himself was selected leader.
(Now *himself* refers to *he*.)

EXAMPLE 3: Incorrect: Himself bought the antique pocket watch.
Correct: He bought the antique pocket watch *himself*.
(*Himself* refers to *he*.)

EXAMPLE 4: Correct: Mother baked the whole-wheat breads *herself*.
(*Herself* refers to *Mother*.)

RULE 9: Use the pronouns *who* and *whom* the same way you would use *he* and *him*. *Who* is like *he* and *whom* is like *him*. (The *m*'s make remembering easy!)

 Hint: Use these three steps to determine correct use of *who* or *whom*:

Step 1: Cross out everything up to *who* or *whom*.
Step 2: Reword the sentence as necessary.
Step 3: Substitute *he* or *him* for *who* or *whom*.

Application 1:

Step 1:	We didn't know (who/whom) could operate the new calculator.
	. . . (who/whom) could operate the new calculator.
Step 2:	(no rewording necessary)

Step 3:   *He* could operate the new calculator.
Solution: We didn't know *who* could operate the new calculator.

Application 2:
Step 1:   I'm not sure (who/whom) you could ask for the money.
             . . . (who/whom) you could ask for the money.
Step 2:   You could ask (who/whom) for the money.
Step 3:   You could ask *him* for the money.
Solution: I'm not sure *whom* you could ask for the money.

RULE 10: Pronouns must agree with the words to which they refer in both number and gender. In other words:

—If the pronoun refers to a singular word, the pronoun must be singular.
—If the pronoun refers to a plural word, the pronoun must be plural.
—If the pronoun refers to a masculine word, the pronoun must be masculine (*he, him, his*).
—If the pronoun refers to a feminine word, the pronoun must be feminine (*she, her, hers*).
—If the pronoun refers to a neuter word, it must be neuter (*it, its, their, theirs, they, them*).

(Obviously, the pronouns *I, we, you,* and *they* in all their forms can be either masculine or feminine.)

EXAMPLE 1:   Each of the workers was at *his* station.
             (Did you remember to watch out for that first prepositional phrase? All the other words are singular; the masculine *his* refers to *each*. Since we do not know whether *each* is masculine or feminine—or a combination—we use the masculine form.)

EXAMPLE 2:   *Neither* of the men brought *his* lunch.
             (*Neither* is singular [refer to Chapter 3, Problem 2], so the pronoun that refers to it is also singular: *his*.)

☞   Hint: Four pronouns can cause peculiar problems in agreement:

                   this, that, these, those

This and *that* are singular and refer to singular words: *this* sort of apple, *that* kind of apple. But *these* and *those* are plural and refer to plural words: *those* kind<u>s</u> of apple<u>s</u>, *these* sort<u>s</u> of apple<u>s</u>. Never use *them* the way you would use *these* and *those: these* apples, not *them* apples.

These ten rules for pronoun usage should solve any problems you may have had concerning correct pronoun usage.

PRACTICE

Exercise 1

Directions: Apply these rules now in practice. When you finish, check your answers with those that follow these sentences. Rule numbers are included so that you can review if you find you still have a problem.

1. Everyone stood at (his/their) seat when the conductor came into the concert hall.

2. Kenneth is braver than (I/me).

3. (We/Us) secretaries must be able to work with numerous kinds of complicated equipment.

4. (This/These) kinds of apples keep well through winter.

5. The award was given jointly by my brother and (I/me).

6. The two automobile drivers, Mr. Johnson and (he/him), appeared in traffic court yesterday morning.

7. The Boy Scouts try to help (whoever/whomever) is in need.

8. (That/Those) sort of wax bean is especially prolific.

9. All of the students were ready with (his/their) papers.

10. Charles bought my sister and (I/me) some medicinal plants for our greenhouse.

11. Organic gardeners object to (your/you) using nonorganic fertilizers and insecticides.

12. The agricultural agent thought (that/those) kind of shrub would be insect resistant.

13. Race-car drivers must keep (his/their) bodies in excellent condition.

14. The guests who were wearing contact lenses were Carl, Gerald, Tommy, and (she/her).

15. (This/These) kind of print is called a *calico* print.

16. Mathilda and (she/her) prepared homemade hominy.

17. The best model-ship builder in this community is (he/him) in the red plaid shirt.

18. The chirping crickets lulled (he/him) and (I/me) to sleep.

19. (He/Himself) collected moths as a hobby.

20. Patricia said that each child had to pick up (his/their) own toys.

21. The nominees for president and vice-president will probably be Mrs. Gallmeister and (I/me) respectively.

22. Shoveling snow in subzero weather delighted neither (he/him) nor (I/me).

23. United Parcel Service delivered a package addressed to (we/us) women in the family.

24. Several workers earn more money than (he/him).

25. The nighthawk objected to (me/my) being near her eggs, which were lying in the gravel of the courtyard.

26. Someone left (her/their) jacket lying on the bench.

27. The barometer was won by a man (who/whom) the neighbors said would enjoy using it.

28. Dad bought a new compact car for (him/himself).

29. The naturalist and (she/her) led our group along a fascinating nature trail.

30. The motorcycle riders selected two riders they themselves thought excellent, Robert and (he/him).

31. Did everybody get all the cake and ice cream (he/they) wanted?

32. The best bread-baker in Vanderburgh County was (she/her).

33. The man (who/whom) they selected to be the speaker was pleased to accept the invitation.

34. Each of the members cast (his/their) ballots for the four officers.

35. The winner will be (he or she/him or her) who has the best attendance record.

Exercise 1—Answers

1. his (Rule 10): *Everyone* is singular.

2. I [am] (Rule 5)

3. We (Rule 4)

4. These (Rule 10)

5. me (Rule 3): *By* is a preposition and needs an object.

6. he (Rule 7): *He* renames part of the subject, *drivers*.

7. whoever (Rule 9): Think "*he* is in need."

8. That (Rule 10)

9. their (Rule 10)

10. me (Rule 3): Charles bought *me* plants.

11. your (Rule 6)

12. that (Rule 10)

13. their (Rule 10)

14. she (Rule 2): The linking verb *were* requires the same form as the subject: *she*.

15. This (Rule 10)

16. she (Rule 1): Think "*she* prepared."

17. he (Rule 2): The linking verb *is* requires the same form as the subject.

18. him and me (Rule 3)

19. He (Rule 8)

20. his (Rule 10): *Each child* is singular and so requires a singular pronoun.

21. I (Rule 2): The linking verb *will be* requires the same form as the subject.

22. him nor me (Rule 3)

23. us (Rule 4)

24. he [did] (Rule 5)

25. my (Rule 6)

26. her (Rule 10): *Someone* is singular and so requires a singular pronoun.

27. who (Rule 9): Think "the neighbors said *he* would enjoy using it."

28. himself (Rule 8)

29. she (Rule 1)

30. him (Rule 7): Think "the riders selected *him*."

31. he (Rule 10): *Everybody* is singular and so requires a singular pronoun.

32. she (Rule 2): Here is another linking verb!

33. whom (Rule 9): Think "they selected *him*."

34. his (Rule 10): *Each* is singular and so requires a singular pronoun. Do not let the prepositional phrase *of the members* interfere.

35. he or she (Rule 2): It is another linking verb!

Exercise 2

Directions: The following passage includes errors in both subject-verb agreement and pronoun usage. Correct the errors and compare your answers with those that follow. Page references will help you review items you miss.

(1) Two crappie fishermen, F. J. Botz and Alan Goodson, have entered the Kingston fishing tournament hoping to land big dollars for theirselves. (2) Since each pair of fishermen work as a team, Botz hopes to have his own boat ready for he and Goodson to launch on tournament day. (3) Although Goodson usually catches more fish than him, Botz prefers his long-time partner to anyone else. (4) "In a tournament situation," Botz explained, "he and I support each other. (5) If he catches the first fish, I cheer him on, and whomever catches the most pounds gets a free dinner from the other." (6) "There is," as Goodson added, however, "also free-dinner rewards for friendly weekend competition between Botz and I." (7) So far, the men agree, the free dinners from tournaments or from weekend fishing is about equal, and each holds their own in a nearly equal pound-for-pound contest. (8) As a result, the two men believe each have a chance at some tournament prizes; but together, these kind of teams should give real competition to the others. (9) If Goodson lands the slab crappie he usually does, the biggest prize may go to himself. (10) According to Roger Yates, tournament chairman, "The final decision, of course, will not be by we tournament judges. (11) The Weights and Measures people from the state will give the final say when he reads the official scales. (12) The scales themselves tell the final story."

Exercise 2—Answers

Sentence 1:

for *themselves* (Rule 8, page 49)

Sentence 2:

pair *works* (Problem 1, Situation A, page 36); for *Goodson and him* (Rule 3, page 47)

Sentence 3:

more than *he* [does] (Rule 5, pages 47–48)

Sentence 4:

(correct)

Sentence 5:

whoever catches (Rule 9, pages 49–50)

Sentence 6:

There *are* rewards (Problem 1, Situation B, page 37); between Botz and *me* (Rule 3, page 47)

Sentence 7:

dinners *are* (Problem 1, Situation A, page 36); each holds *his* own (Rule 10, page 50)

Sentence 8:

each *has* (Problem 2, Group A, pages 37–38); these *kinds* [or *this* kind of *team*] (Rule 10, page 50)

Sentence 9:

prize may go to *him* (Rule 8, page 49)

Sentence 10:

by *us* judges (Rule 4, page 47)

Sentence 11:

when *they read* (Rule 10, page 50)

Sentence 12:

(correct)

5

ADJECTIVE AND ADVERB USAGE

Usage errors can occur when choosing between an adjective and an adverb form. Should you say, "I don't feel good" or "I don't feel well"? "I feel bad" or "I feel badly"? To help solve adjective and adverb usage problems, remember two rules from Chapter 1:

1. Adjectives must modify *nouns*.
2. Adverbs must modify *verbs*, *adjectives*, or other *adverbs*.

Nine rules will help solve other adjective and adverb problems:

RULES

RULE 1: Use adverbs to modify action verbs.

   EXAMPLE: Harold drives his new car *carefully*.
   (*Carefully*, an adverb, modifies the action verb *drives*.)

RULE 2: Use adverbs to modify adjectives.

   EXAMPLE: We thought the test was *really* (not *real*) difficult.
   (*Really*, an adverb, modifies the adjective *difficult*.)

RULE 3: Use an adjective after a linking verb. (Remember, substitute some form of *to be* to test for a linking verb.)

   EXAMPLE 1:   The owner of the automobile appeared angry.
   (*Appeared* is a linking verb: *The owner of the automobile is angry.* So we need the adjective *angry*.)

   EXAMPLE 2:   The owner of the car appeared *suddenly*.
   (Now *appeared* is an action verb. You cannot say, *The owner of the car is suddenly.* So, since *appeared* is an action verb, you must use the adverb *suddenly*. See Rule 1.)

RULE 4: *Bad* is an adjective; *badly* is an adverb. Use the adjective, *bad*, after the linking verb.

   EXAMPLE 1:   He feels *bad*.
   (*Feels* is a linking verb and so requires the adjective *bad*.)

55

EXAMPLE 2:   The repairman did a *bad* job on the car.
(*Bad* functions as an adjective to modify the noun *job*.)

EXAMPLE 3:   The inexperienced actor performed *badly* even in the small role.
(*Badly* functions as an adverb to modify the verb *performed*.)

RULE 5:   *Good* is an adjective; *well* can be an adjective *or* an adverb.

When *well* is an adjective, it means

a. in good health
b. of good appearance
c. satisfactory

NOTE: Usually, *well* as an adjective is used after a linking verb.

EXAMPLE 1:   Charlie did a *good* job welding the lawnmower handle back in place.
(*Good* is an adjective modifying the noun *job*.)

EXAMPLE 2:   Mother looks *well* in that dress.
(*Well* here is an adjective meaning "of good appearance" after a linking verb, *looks*.)

EXAMPLE 3:   He did the job *well*.
(*Well* is now used as an adverb modifying the action verb *did*.)

EXAMPLE 4:   All is well.
(*Well* is an adjective meaning "satisfactory" after the linking verb *is*.)

EXAMPLE 5:   I don't feel *well*.
(*Well* is an adjective meaning "in good health" after the linking verb *do feel*.)

RULE 6:   Use *fewer* to refer to countable things and *less* to refer to amounts.

EXAMPLE 1:   The recipe calls for *less* sugar than vinegar.
(You cannot count sugar: one sugar, two sugars.)

EXAMPLE 2:   My recipe calls for *fewer* cups of sugar than yours does.
(You *can* counts cups of sugar: one cup of sugar, two cups of sugar.)

EXAMPLE 3:   Bob has *less* money than Gino.
(You *cannot* count money: one money, two monies.)

EXAMPLE 4:   Bob has fewer dollar bills than Gino.
(You *can* count dollar bills: one dollar bill, two dollar bills.)

☞   Hint: Anytime you use *fewer* or *less*, be sure to say fewer or less *than what*.

EXAMPLE   Incorrect: The oak tree has fewer leaves.
Correct: The oak tree has fewer leaves *than the maple tree*.

RULE 7: Distinguish between the comparative and the superlative forms.

> **Part A.** If you are discussing *two* things, use the comparative form of the adjective or adverb. (The comparative form ends in *-er* or uses the word *more*.)
>
>> EXAMPLE 1: Paul is the *older* one of the two brothers.
>>
>> EXAMPLE 2: Tex is the *more handsome* of the two actors.
>
> **Part B.** If you are discussing more than two, use the superlative form. (The superlative form ends in *-est* or uses the word *most*.)
>
>> EXAMPLE 1: Aunt Mary is the *tallest* one of the three sisters.
>>
>> EXAMPLE 2: Katherine is the *most energetic* of the group.

RULE 8: Avoid double negatives.

> EXAMPLE 1: Incorrect: We *didn't* do *no* homework.
> Correct: We didn't do any homework.
>
> EXAMPLE 2: Incorrect: *There aren't hardly* any good building sites left there anymore.
> Correct: There are hardly any good building sites left there anymore.

RULE 9: Avoid illogical comparisons.

> EXAMPLE: Illogical: Quincy is taller than any student in his class. (But since Quincy is, obviously, in his own class, you are saying that he is taller than himself!)
> Better: Quincy is taller than any *other* student in his class.

These nine rules, when applied correctly, should keep you out of trouble with adjective and adverb usage. Check, now, to see if you understand.

PRACTICE

Exercise 1

Directions: Check yourself on the practice below. If you miss an item, be sure to go back to the rule and study the examples for further clarification. Rule numbers are given with the answers following these sentences.

1. The medicated lotion was (good/well) for bee stings.
2. Marjorie felt (bad/badly) about having embarrassed her dear friend.
3. The mongrel appeared (happy/happily) lying there on the velvet cushion.
4. When in training, our neighbor runs four miles a day (regular/regularly).
5. Lately, our winters have been (real/really) cold.
6. The leg was broken (bad/badly).
7. Compared with my brother, I am the (taller/tallest) one.
8. I have little patience, but she has even (fewer/less).
9. The caterers (didn't hardly have/hardly had) enough food for everyone.
10. Clovis won more awards than (anyone/anyone else) in his sales district.
11. The vice-president of the group is the (more/most) assertive of the officers.
12. There are (fewer/less) cars in the parking lot now than there were at noon.
13. After being sick yesterday, Father says he is feeling (good/well) today.
14. The situation appeared (bad/badly).
15. The holiday was a (delightful/delightfully) beautiful day.
16. The colors in the five-piece outfit went together (good/well).
17. There are three of us girls in the family, and Sue Ellen is the (older/oldest) one of my sisters.
18. The child behaved (bad/badly).
19. The job was done (good/well).
20. Marilyn looks (good/well) with her hair cut short.

Exercise 1—Answers

1. good (Rule 5)
2. bad (Rule 4): *Felt* is a linking verb.
3. happy (Rule 3): *Appeared* is a linking verb.
4. regularly (Rule 1)
5. really (Rule 2): *Really*, the adverb, is required to modify the predicate adjective *cold*.
6. badly (Rule 4): *Badly* modifies the action verb *was broken*.
7. taller (Rule 7)
8. less (Rule 6)
9. hardly had (Rule 8)
10. anyone else (Rule 9)

11. most (Rule 7)

12. fewer (Rule 6)

13. well (Rule 5): The adjective *well* is used here to mean "in good health."

14. bad (Rule 4): *Appeared* is a linking verb.

15. delightfully (Rule 2)

16. well (Rule 5): *Well* is used as an adverb to modify the action verb *went.*

17. older (Rule 7): Bet you goofed! If there are three of us, then I have only two sisters.

18. badly (Rule 4): *Badly* modifies the action verb *behaved.*

19. well (Rule 5): The adverb modifies the action verb *was done.*

20. well (Rule 5): The adjective means "of good appearance."

Exercise 2

Directions: The following passage includes a mixture of errors: subject-verb agreement, pronoun usage, and adjective-adverb usage. Apply your understanding of the rules to correct the errors. Then check your answers below. Page references will help you review problem areas.

(1) Today's children, for whom science makes life good, need read only digital clocks. (2) In my opinion, that's a real sad situation. (3) Of course, my critics will say that reading "8:45" takes less words than reading "fifteen minutes until nine." (4) On the other hand, every child should know what us adults mean by "quarter 'til nine." (5) How can these children understand "quarter past" or "half hour" by merely reading horizontal numbers? (6) Neither the children nor I are able to talk about matters as simple as bedtime or dinner hour without confusion! (7) Even if mathematics is the child's best subject, the digital clock will never help them understand our traditional-clock vocabulary.

Exercise 2—Answers

Sentence 1:

  (correct)

Sentence 2:

  really sad (Rule 2, page 55)

Sentence 3:

  fewer words (Rule 6, page 56)

Sentence 4:

  we adults (Rule 4, page 47)

Sentence 5:

  (correct)

Sentence 6:

  children nor I *am* (Problem 3, Situation C, page 39)

Sentence 7:

  never help *him* (or *her*) [referring to *child's*] (Rule 10, page 50)

6
TROUBLESOME VERBS

Irregular verbs often create problems. Your dictionary will solve most of these problems. Three pairs of verbs, however, create special problems because the verbs in each pair look so much alike:

Present	Past	Participle (Test with *has*, *have*, or *had*)	Progressive
sit	sat	sat	sitting
set	set	set	setting
rise	rose	risen	rising
raise	raised	raised	raising
lie	lay	lain	lying
lay	laid	laid	laying

SPECIAL PROBLEM-VERBS

Pair 1: Sit/Set
Sit means "to rest," as in a chair.
Set means "to put or place."

EXAMPLES: The team members will *sit* together.
The team members will *set* their goals.

NOTE: *Sit* will not take a direct object. *Set must* have a direct object, either stated or implied. So anytime you use the word *set*, there must be an answer to the question, "Set *who* or *what?*"

Pair 2: Rise/Raise
Rise, like *sit*, will not take a direct object.
Raise, like *set*, must have a direct object.

EXAMPLE 1:   The window *rises* mysteriously.
(no direct object)

EXAMPLE 2:   Please *raise* the windows!
Ask, "Raise *who* or *what?*" Answer: *windows*

EXAMPLE 3:   The bread dough *rose* almost double in an hour.
(no direct object)

EXAMPLE 4:   That truck farmer *raises* especially beautiful produce.
Ask, "Raises *who* or *what?*" Answer: *produce*.

Pair 3:   Lie/Lay

Lie means to rest or recline, and, like *rise* and *sit*, will not take a direct object. *Lay* means to put or place, and, like *raise* and *set*, it *must* have a direct object.

What makes these two verbs so confusing is that *lay* in the present is the same as *lie* in the past:

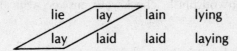

lie   lay   lain   lying

lay   laid   laid   laying

☞   Hint: To help you select the correct word, test by substituting "rest or recline" for the forms of *lie* and "put or place" for the forms of *lay*.

EXAMPLE 1:   (Lie/Lay) the baby in her crib.
Substitute: Put or place the baby in her crib.
Solution: *Lay* the baby in her crib.

EXAMPLE 2:   (Laying/Lying) in the sun can cause unfortunate side effects.
Substitute: Resting or reclining in the sun can cause unfortunate side effects.
Solution: *Lying* in the sun can cause unfortunate side effects.

Summary

s(i)t
r(i)se   } have *no* direct objects
l(i)e

(Think of *i* as representing *i*ndependent: not dependent on a direct object for existence!)

set
raise   } *must* have direct objects
lay

PRACTICE

Exercise 1

Directions: Check your understanding of these three pairs of verbs by working through the following sentences. When you finish, check your answers with those that follow these sentences.

1. When I finish raking the lawn, I plan to (lay/lie) down for a nap.

2. Grandpa always (set/sat) in a high-backed wicker rocker.

3. The temperature and our tempers were both (raising/rising).

4. "He can't come to the phone," she explained; "he's just (laid/lain) down."

5. The gardener was (sitting/setting) tomato plants in three one-hundred-foot rows.

6. The family pet, a dog of mixed descent, (lay/laid) in front of the television set.

7. (Lying/Laying) flat on his back, the football player appeared to be injured.

8. The group did exercises in a (sitting/setting) position.

9. The doctor's report (raised/rose) the family's hopes.

10. Those old newspapers have (lain/laid) there for three weeks now.

11. Citizens watched in helpless frustration as the flood waters (raised/rose).

12. Please (sit/set) the baby in this chair, not that one.

13. The big Persian cat, (laying/lying) in the open window, dozed peacefully.

14. Come and (set/sit) with us!

15. The toys were (laying/lying) along the edge of the driveway.

Exercise 1—Answers

1. lie (no direct object; substitute *rest*)

2. sat (no direct object)

3. rising (no direct object)

4. lain (no direct object; substitute *reclined*)

5. setting (direct object: plants)

6. lay (no direct object; substitute *rested*)

7. Lying (no direct object; substitute *reclining*)

8. sitting (no direct object)

9. raised (direct object: hopes)

10. lain (no direct object; substitute *reclined*)

11. rose (no direct object)

12. set (direct object: baby)

13. lying (no direct object; substitute *resting*)

14. sit (no direct object)

15. lying (no direct object; substitute *reclining*)

Exercise 2

Directions: Now apply your understanding to the following passage and correct the errors. Compare your answers with the answers below.

(1) At 6:15 when I came in, Jennifer, the cat, was laying curled on the couch asleep. (2) As usual I set in my chair to read the day's mail and glance at the paper. (3) After a lapse of time, however, for no apparent reason I felt suddenly compelled to put down my paper and study the cat; for setting there, it occurred to me that she lay too quietly too long. (4) I raised from my chair, lay the paper on the seat, and walked toward her. (5) I studied her carefully, noting how her tail lay over her nose without a hair stirring. (6) I watched her side, trying to distinguish the slightest rise or fall of her rib cage, but I could see nothing. (7) I called her name. (8) A whisker moved; an eyelid raised; one paw stretched; but her tail laid carefully curled across her nose. (9) Ah, that I could take such cat naps!

Exercise 2—Answers

Sentence 1:

lying (no direct object)

Sentence 2:

sat (no direct object)

Sentence 3:

sitting (no direct object)

Sentence 4:

rose (no direct object); laid (direct object: paper)

Sentence 8:

rose (no direct object); lay (no direct object)

(Sentences 5, 6, 7, and 9 are correct.)

III

PHRASES AND CLAUSES

7

VERBALS

You can get through life quite comfortably without knowing anything about verbals. In fact, verbals function as nouns, adjectives, or adverbs; so, in essence, you already know about them from Chapter 1. Why, then, spend any time talking about them? For the purposes of the GED, there is one main reason: understanding some of the basics about verbals will make understanding punctuation much easier. For the purposes of improving your writing, there is a secondary reason. Knowing how to use verbals will improve your ability to vary sentence structure. (There were three verbals in that last sentence, by the way!)

Verbals are words that look like verbs but are not used as verbs. Verbals can be used as nouns, adjectives, or adverbs; so they can function in the following ways:

subjects
direct objects
objects of prepositions
predicate words
appositives
noun modifiers
verb modifiers
adjective modifiers
adverb modifiers

We will talk about the characteristics and functions of the three kinds of verbals:

infinitives
gerunds
participles

PART 1: INFINITIVES

A. Characteristics: An infinitive has the following characteristics to help you recognize it:

1. Basic appearance: An infinitive is made up of *to* plus a verb.

   EXAMPLE 1:   *To sing* is his goal. (*To* plus the verb *sing* makes the infinitive.)
   EXAMPLE 2:   He wanted *to work* late. (*To* and the verb *work* makes the infinitive.)

2. Infinitive phrase: Verbals, like verbs, take both adverb modifiers and direct objects. The infinitive and its objects and/or modifiers form the infinitive phrase. (Remember that objects answer *who?* or *what?* after the verbal; adverb modifiers tell *how, when, where,* or *to what extent.*)

EXAMPLE: He wanted *to drive the borrowed car carefully*. (*To* and the verb *drive* make the infinitive. If you ask, "To drive *who* or *what?*," you get *car* as your answer. That, of course, is the object of the infinitive *to drive*. *Carefully* tells *how* about the infinitive *to drive*, so it is an adverb modifier. The entire infinitive phrase, then, is *to drive the borrowed car carefully*.

To put it simply:

$$\text{to } + \text{ verb } + \left\{ \begin{array}{l} \text{object(s)} \\ \text{and/or} \\ \text{modifier(s)} \end{array} \right\} = \text{infinitive phrase}$$

Now consider this additional example:

EXAMPLE: To instruct his young relatives in the routines of square dancing was the fiddler's only desire.

Infinitive: *to instruct (to* + the verb *instruct)*
Object: *relatives* (Instruct *who* or *what?*)
Modifiers: *young* (adjective modifying the object *relatives);* *in the routines* (prepositional phrase that modifies instruct); and *of square danc- ing* (prepositional phrase that modifies *routines)*

The entire infinitive phrase, then, is *to instruct his young relatives in the rou- tines of square dancing.*

 Warning: Remember that not every *to* will introduce an infinitive.

to + noun   = prepositional phrase
to + verb   = infinitive

EXAMPLE 1:   He walked to the concert hall early. (*To the concert hall* is *to* plus the noun *hall* and so is a prepositional phrase, not an infinitive.)
EXAMPLE 2:   He walked to keep trim. (*To keep trim* is *to* plus the verb *keep* and therefore an infinitive.

B. **Function:** An infinitive or infinitive phrase functions as a noun or as an adjective or as an adverb. Think of the whole phrase as one word. You can then use the sen- tence-attack plan to determine which part of the sentence it is. (See Chapter 2.) If the infinitive does not fit in the sentence-attack plan, then you know you have a modifier.

Consider now the specific functions of an infinitive:

1. Noun: Since an infinitive functions as a noun, it can function in most of the ways a noun can function:

   a. As subject

   EXAMPLE: *To become educated* was their primary ambition. (*To become educated* is the subject of *was.)*

   b. As predicate word

   EXAMPLE: The program's purpose was *to entertain*. (*To entertain* follows the linking verb *was* and renames the subject *purpose.)*

    c. As an appositive

        EXAMPLE: While in college, Marlene had only one goal: *to get as thorough an education as possible.* (Remember that an appositive renames a noun. *To get as thorough an education as possible* renames *goal.*)

    d. As direct object

        EXAMPLE: The City Councilman wanted *to expand the Park Board budget.* (*To expand the Park Board budget* answers *what?* after the action verb *wanted.*)

2. Adjective: As an adjective, an infinitive modifies a noun:

   EXAMPLE: This is the class *to take!* (*To take* modifies the noun *class.*)

3. Adverb: Like other adverbs, infinitives can modify verbs, adjectives, and other adverbs:

    a. As verb modifier

        EXAMPLE: Martha has gone *to visit her sister in New Orleans.* (*To visit her sister in New Orleans* answers the adverb question *where?* about the action verb *gone.*)

    b. As adjective modifier

        EXAMPLE: You were lucky *to pass the course.* (*To pass the course* explains *how* about the predicate adjective *lucky.*)

    c. As adverb modifier

        EXAMPLE: The doctor operated too late *to save the accident victim.* (*To save the accident victim* explains *to what extent* about the adverb *late.*)

C. ***"To*-less" infinitive:** Sometimes the infinitive appears without the word *to.*

   EXAMPLE: May I help you bake the cookies?
                (*Bake the cookies,* a "*to*-less" infinitive, is the direct object of *help.*)

D. **Process:** Use the following steps to identify the function of the infinitive phrase:

   Step 1:   Identify the phrase.
   Step 2:   Think of the phrase as one word.
   Step 3:   Use the sentence-attack plan to determine the functions of subject, direct object, and predicate word.
   Step 4:   If the phrase does not fit in the sentence-attack plan, you will know the phrase is a modifier.

   EXAMPLE 1:   The incumbent hoped to win the election.

   Step 1:   The incumbent hoped *to win the election.*
   Step 2:   Think: The incumbent hoped towintheelection.
   Step 3:   a.   Find the verb: *hoped*
              b.   *Hoped* is an action verb.

     c. Ask: *who* or *what* hoped?
       Answer: *incumbent* (subject)
     d. Ask: incumbent hoped *who* or *what?*
       Answer: *towintheelection*
       (The infinitive phrase is the direct object.)

EXAMPLE 2: The man *to see about gardening problems* is the county agent.

Step 1:   The man *to see about gardening problems* is the county agent.
Step 2:   Think: The man *toseeaboutgardeningproblems* is the county agent.
Step 3:   a. Find the verb: *is*
          b. *Is* is a linking verb.
          c. Ask: *who* or *what is?*
             Answer: *man* (subject)
          d. Ask: man is *who* or *what?*
             Answer: *agent* (predicate noun)
Step 4:   The infinitive did not fit in the sentence-attack plan, so it must be a modifier. *To see about gardening problems* answers *which one* about the noun *man,* so the infinitive phrase functions as an adjective.

E. **Usage:** As you begin consciously using infinitive phrases to increase sentence variety, keep in mind that the *to* and the verb form should not be separated:

EXAMPLE: Incorrect: He planned *to* not *go* on a vacation this year.
           Correct: He planned not *to go* on a vacation this year.

The separation of *to* from the verb form is called a *split infinitive.* Effective writers try to avoid split infinitives.

PART 2: GERUNDS

A. **Characteristics:** A gerund has the following characteristics:

1. Basic appearance: A gerund ends in *-ing*.

EXAMPLE 1: *Swimming* at Hartke Pool is his favorite pastime.
EXAMPLE 2: *Running* weekend marathons in the city keeps him in good physical shape.
EXAMPLE 3: He considered *running* for office.
EXAMPLE 4: After *eating* the cake and ice cream, I felt stuffed.

2. Gerund phrases: Gerunds, like infinitives, can take objects and modifiers. All of these together make up the gerund phrase:

$$\left. \begin{array}{c} \textit{-ing} \text{ word} \\ + \\ \text{object(s)} \\ + \\ \text{modifier(s)} \end{array} \right\} = \text{gerund phrase}$$

EXAMPLE 1: *Swimming at Hartke Pool* is his favorite pastime.
               (*At Hartke Pool* modifies *swimming* by explaining *where.* So the entire gerund phrase is the gerund plus its modifier: *swimming at Hartke Pool.*)

EXAMPLE 2:   *Running weekend marathons in the city* keeps him in good physical shape.
(*Marathons* answers *what?* about *running,* so it is the object of the gerund. *Weekend* describes *which* about *marathons. In the city,* a prepositional phrase, functions as an adverb to tell *where* about *marathons.* The gerund and its object and modifiers, then, make up the entire gerund phrase: *running weekend marathons in the city.*)

EXAMPLE 3:   He considered *running for office.*
(*For office* tells *how?* about *running,* so the gerund phrase is *running for office.*)

EXAMPLE 4:   After *eating the cake and ice cream,* I felt stuffed.
(*Cake and ice cream* answer *what?* after *eating. Cake and ice cream* are the compound objects of the gerund *eating.* They and the gerund make up the complete gerund phrase: *eating the cake and ice cream.*)

⟹   Warning: Not all *-ing* words are gerunds. With that warning in mind, think about *function.*

B.   **Function:** A gerund or a gerund phrase functions as a noun. (Remember, think of the phrase as a single word.)

1. As subject

EXAMPLE: *Playing flag football* was not his idea of fun.
(*Playing flag football* is the subject of *was.*)

2. As predicate word

EXAMPLE: Aunt Mary's hobby is *crocheting doilies.*
(*Crocheting doilies* answers *what?* after the linking verb *is* and renames the subject *hobby.*)

3. As direct object

EXAMPLE: Most people enjoy *listening to music.*
(*Listening to music* answers *what?* after the action verb *enjoy.*)

4. As object of the preposition

EXAMPLE: The attorney won the case by *proving the witness a liar.*
(*By* is a preposition, and *proving the witness a liar* answers *by what?* The whole prepositional phrase functions to tell *how?* about the verb *won.*)

5. As appositive

EXAMPLE: His job, *collecting data for the Environmental Protection Agency,* required painstaking effort.
(Remember, an appositive, which renames another noun, is usually set off with commas. This gerund phrase, which functions as an appositive, renames the noun *job.*)

Now let us reconsider the Warning: Not all *-ing* words are gerunds. Which of the following *-ing* words are gerunds?

1. Robert is *swimming* forty laps a day, now.
2. The small child, *walking* alone, became lost.
3. *Sobbing*, the old woman sank to her knees.
4. Woolen garments are *rising* in price.
5. The puppy was *chewing* on my shoes for two days.

None of these *-ing* words are gerunds. Why? None of them function as *nouns*. Look at the following explanations:

1. *Is swimming* is the verb.
2. *Walking* functions as an adjective.
3. *Sobbing* functions as an adjective.
4. *Are rising* is the verb.
5. *Was chewing* is the verb.

 Remember: *Function* tells all. To be gerunds, *-ing* words must function as *nouns*.

PART 3: PARTICIPLES

A. **Characteristics:** Participles have the following characteristics to help you recognize them:

1. Basic appearance: Because there are two kinds of participles, they have two different forms:

   a. Past participles usually end in *-ed* (the form of the verb you would use with the helping words *have* or *has*: have *walked*, have *taken*, have *sung*.)

   EXAMPLE: The picture frame, *mottled* with old paint, needed refinishing.

   b. Present participles end in *-ing*. (So they *look* like gerunds. They do *not*, however, function as gerunds do.)

   EXAMPLE 1:   The picture *hanging* above the sofa depicts a pastoral scene.
   (A present participle functioning as an adjective to modify the noun *picture*)
   EXAMPLE 2:   Warren likes *walking* for daily exercise.
   (A gerund functioning as a noun, the object of the verb *likes*)

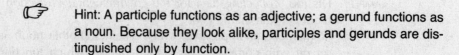 Hint: A participle functions as an adjective; a gerund functions as a noun. Because they look alike, participles and gerunds are distinguished only by function.

2. Participial phrases: Just like infinitives and gerunds, participles can have objects and modifiers.

$$\left. \begin{array}{c} \text{participle} \\ + \\ \text{object(s)} \\ + \\ \text{modifier(s)} \end{array} \right\} = \text{participial phrase}$$

a. As present participial phrase

EXAMPLE 1: *Walking home from work*, John tripped on the sidewalk.
(*Home* tells *where* about *walking;* and *from work*, a prepositional phrase, modifies *walking*. The whole phrase, then, is the participle plus its modifiers: *walking home from work*.)

EXAMPLE 2: *Singing a haunting melody*, the soloist won the audience's approval.
(*Melody* answers *what?* about *singing*, so it is the object of the participle. *Haunting* tells *what kind* about *melody*. So the whole participial phrase is *singing a haunting melody*.)

b. As past participial phrase

EXAMPLE: *Beaten by the wind*, the tomato plants looked wilted.
(*By the wind* tells *how* about *beaten;* then the whole participial phrase is made of the participle and its modifier: *beaten by the wind*.)

B. Function: Participles always function as adjectives. They modify nouns. As adjectives, participles may serve in the following ways:

1. Noun modifier

EXAMPLE 1: *Walking down the road*, we saw a fox terrier.
(The participle modifies the subject *we*.)

EXAMPLE 2: We saw a fox terrier *walking down the road*.
(The participle modifies the object *terrier*.)

2. Predicate word

EXAMPLE 1: The supervisor was *mistaken*.
(*Mistaken* follows the linking verb *was* and describes the subject *supervisor*.)

EXAMPLE 2: The defendant seemed *unconcerned about the attorney's questioning*.
(The participial phrase follows the linking verb *seemed* and describes the subject *defendant*.)

C. Usage: When the participial phrase appears at the beginning of a sentence, the phrase is followed by a comma. The phrase will modify the noun immediately after the comma.

EXAMPLE: *Watching the sunrise from inside their tent*, the two campers reveled in their enjoyment of the peace and quiet.
(The participial phrase, followed by a comma, modifies *campers*, the first noun after the comma.)

Warning: Since the participial phrase *must* modify the first noun after the comma, be sure to avoid ridiculous sentences:

EXAMPLE 1: Ridiculous: Arriving late at the bus stop, the bus went off without me.
(The *bus* did not arrive late!)

Better: Arriving late at the bus stop, I missed the bus.
(The participial phrase must modify the noun after the comma: *I*.)

EXAMPLE 2: Ridiculous: Having forgotten to wind it, the clock stopped at midnight.
(The *clock* did not forget to wind itself!)

Better: Having forgotten to wind the clock, I found it had stopped at midnight.

EXAMPLE 3: Ridiculous: Walking home from the graveyard, an old abandoned house seemed especially eerie.
(A *house* walking??)

Better: Walking home from the graveyard, Robert thought the old abandoned house seemed especially eerie.

PRACTICE

Exercise 1

Directions: Look at the following sentences and find the verbals. Identify the kind of verbal (infinitive, gerund, or participle) and its function (subject, modifier of noun, predicate word, etc.). Answers appear following the sentences. See if you really understand. Hint: *Some sentences have more than one verbal.*

1. Startled, he stood quietly, breathing rapidly.

2. An excellent form of exercise is jogging at a steady, even pace for a mile or so.

3. To find the old cemetery, we followed the nearly invisible trail; but, suffering from the heat, we gave up.

4. To eat moderately seemed advisable.

5. Washing a car is sometimes tedious to do.

6. The old man's hobby was playing in a German folk band.

7. After the heavy snows ceased, I no longer wished to be confined to the house.

8. The try-outs, conducted by the orchestra director and her assistant, were held once each year.

9. Sustained by chocolate, I shall win all battles except those with the waistline.

10. Having refused his phone call, Evelyn had little chance of accepting his apology.

Exercise 1—Answers

1. *Startled* is a participle and functions as an adjective to modify the noun *he. Breathing rapidly* is a participial phrase and functions to modify the noun *he.* (Remember, participles can modify only *nouns,* not verbs.)

2. *Jogging at a steady, even pace for a mile or so* is a gerund phrase and is the predicate word after the linking verb *is.*

3. *To find the old cemetery* is an infinitive phrase and functions as an adverb to modify the verb *followed. Suffering from the heat* is a participial phrase and functions as an adjective to modify the noun *we.*

4. *To eat moderately* is an infinitive phrase and is the subject of the sentence.

5. *Washing a car* is a gerund phrase and is the subject of the sentence. *To do* is an infinitive and functions as an adverb to modify the adjective *tedious.*

6. *Playing in a German folk band* is a gerund phrase and is the predicate word after the linking verb *was.*

7. *To be confined to the house* is an infinitive phrase; and, in a noun function, it is the direct object of the verb *wished.*

8. *Conducted by the orchestra director and her assistant* is a participial phrase and functions as an adjective to modify the noun *try-outs.*

9. *Sustained by chocolate* is a participial phrase and functions as an adjective to modify the noun *I.*

10. *Having refused his phone call* is a participial phrase and functions as an adjective to modify the noun *Evelyn. Accepting his apology* is a gerund phrase; and, acting as a noun, it is the object of the preposition *of.*

8

CLAUSES

There are two kinds of clauses:

1. independent clauses (sometimes called main clauses) with subjects and verbs that can stand alone as sentences
2. dependent clauses (sometimes called subordinate clauses), which have subjects and verbs but cannot stand alone.

> EXAMPLES: ... after the *snow began*....
> ... *that stands* in the front yard....
> ... that *I told* you about....

Notice that clauses are different from phrases in that clauses *must* have subjects and verbs; phrases do not have subjects and verbs. (You will learn more about independent and dependent clauses in Chapter 15.)

There are three kinds of dependent clauses that we will be studying in this chapter:

1. noun clause
2. adjective clause
3. adverb clause

PART 1: NOUN CLAUSE

A. Characteristics:

1. The noun clause will have a subject and a verb and will usually start with one of these words:

who	which
whose	what
whom	that

(*Ever* can be added to most of these words, too: *whoever, whatever*.)

EXAMPLE 1: That man is *who came to the door*.
(Subject, *who*; verb, *came*)
EXAMPLE 2: No one knew *whose book was left behind*.
(Subject, *book*; verb, *was left*)
EXAMPLE 3: I talked with *whomever the company sent to settle my claim*.
(Subject, *company*; verb, *sent*)
EXAMPLE 4: *Which party is guilty* is the question.
(Subject, *party*; verb, *is*)

76

EXAMPLE 5:   There is no excuse for *what happened.*
             (Subject, *what*; verb, *happened*)
EXAMPLE 6:   Brad explained *that Jim's work was done exceptionally well.*
             (Subject, *work*; verb, *was done*)

2. Sometimes the first word in the noun clause is the subject of the verb of the clause.

   EXAMPLE: . . . who came to the door. . . .
              (*Who* is the subject of the verb *came*.)

3. The clause may have an object and/or modifiers.

   EXAMPLE 1:   . . . who came *to the door.* . . .
               (*To the door*, a prepositional phrase, tells *where* about *came*, so the phrase is an adverb modifier.)
   EXAMPLE 2:   *Whoever designed the building* took credit for its striking appearance.
               (*Building* answers *what?* after the action verb *designed*, so it is the direct object of *designed*.)

4. Sometimes the first word in the noun clause is the object of the verb or a predicate word.

   EXAMPLE 1:   *What he saw* startled him.
               (*He* is the subject of the action verb *saw*; *what* is the direct object of *saw*.)
   EXAMPLE 2:   No one knew *who she was.*
               (*Who* is the predicate word after the linking verb *was*.)

B. **Function:**   The noun clause may function many of the same ways a single noun functions:

   1. As subject

      EXAMPLE: *Whoever called you yesterday* mispronounced your name.
                 (The noun clause, when thought of as a single word, answers *who?* in front of the verb.)

   2. As predicate word

      EXAMPLE: His faith is *what keeps him alive.*
                 (The noun clause follows the linking verb *is* and renames *faith*. Notice that the sentence order can be reversed so that the noun clause becomes the subject: *What keeps him alive* is his faith.)

   3. As direct object

      EXAMPLE: The witness explained *what he saw.*
                 (The noun clause answers *what?* after the action verb *explained*.)

   4. As object of preposition

      EXAMPLE: Unfortunately, people are sometimes judged by *what they wear.*
                 (*By* is a preposition, and the noun clause, when thought of as a single word, answers the question *by what?*)

5. As appositive

EXAMPLE: My long-range concern, *that you learn grammar*, helps me to keep finding examples!
(The noun clause renames the noun *concern* and is set off with commas.)

C. **Attack plan:** Use the following steps to determine the function of the noun clause.

Step 1: Find the clause, beginning with one of the special words (*who, whose, whom, which, what,* or *that*) and ending after all the modifiers and/or objects.

Step 2: Think of the clause as a single word.

Step 3: Use the sentence-attack plan (see Chapter 2) to determine how the noun is used. (An appositive will rename, remember, and so will not fit in the sentence-attack plan.)

EXAMPLE: What happens next remains to be seen.

Step 1: Find the clause: *what happens next* (*What* is the subject of the verb *happens*; *next* tells *when* about *happens*.)

Step 2: Think of the clause as one word:
Whathappensnext remains to be seen.

Step 3: Use the sentence-attack plan:
a. Find the verb: *remains*
b. *Remains* is a linking verb. (You can substitute *is*, a form of *to be*.)
c. *Who* or *what* remains?
Answer: *whathappensnext*

So, the noun clause is the *subject* of the sentence.

PART 2: ADJECTIVE CLAUSE

A. **Characteristics:** The adjective clause will have a subject and a verb and will usually start with one of these words:

who whose whom
which that

Sometimes, *when* and *where* can introduce adjective clauses.

EXAMPLE 1: The athlete *who won the Best Sportsmanship Award* was captain of her basketball team.
(Subject, *who*; verb, *won*)

EXAMPLE 2: The lucky person *whose name is drawn* will win a three-day vacation in Miami.
(Subject, *name*; verb, *is drawn*)

EXAMPLE 3: The sidewalk artist could draw a caricature of any famous person *whom you could name.*
(Subject, *you*; verb, *could name*)

EXAMPLE 4: My brother ate all the strawberries *that I picked.*
(Subject, *I*; verb, *picked*)

EXAMPLE 5: We reminisced about the time *when we celebrated our childhood birthdays*.
(Subject, *we*; verb, *celebrated*)

EXAMPLE 6: This is the place *where the accident happened*.
(Subject, *accident*; verb, *happened*)

B. Function: The adjective clause functions the same way a single adjective functions: it answers *which one? what kind?* or *how many?* about a noun.

EXAMPLE: The flower arrangement *that was judged Best of Show* was made up of dried cornshuck flowers.
(*That was judged Best of Show* says *which* about *arrangement*; the clause functions as an adjective modifying the noun *arrangement*.)

C. Attack plan: Since the adjective clause and the noun clause can begin with many of the same words, you will need to consider *function* in order to know whether the clause is an adjective or noun clause.

 Remember: If you use the sentence-attack plan, the *noun* clause will fit into the plan at some point (with the single exception of the appositive). So, if you finish all steps in the sentence-attack plan and have found no use for the clause, you can be fairly certain that the clause is a *modifier*.

EXAMPLE: The boy *whose jacket is lying on the ground* is playing tennis in the second court.
(*Jacket* is the subject of *is lying; on the ground* is a prepositional phrase that tells *where* about *is lying; whose* is possessive and modifies *jacket*.)

Sentence-attack plan:

Step 1: Cross out *in the second court* (prepositional phrase).
Step 2: *Is playing* is the action verb.
Step 3: *Who* or *what* is playing?
Answer: *boy* (subject)
Step 4: Boy is playing *who* or *what*?
Answer: *tennis* (direct object)
Step 5: Boy is playing tennis *to whom* or *for whom*?
Answer: none

So what remains is a modifier. Remember that you must think of the clause as if it were one word. *Whosejacketislyingontheground* tells *which* about the noun *boy*; so the clause is an adjective.

 Warning: Sometimes the clue word (especially the word *that*) is not included:

EXAMPLE: Here is the house *I told you about*.
(*[That] I told you about* is the adjective clause.)

☞   Hint 1: People sometimes confuse <u>who</u>, <u>which</u>, and <u>that</u>.

a. *Who* (or *whom* or *whose*) refers to people.

   EXAMPLE: He is the politician *who* made all those promises.

b. *Which* refers to things or non-human animals.

   EXAMPLE 1:   This tree, *which* stands taller than any others nearby, provides
   shade for both of our yards.
   (*Which* refers to the thing *tree*.)
   EXAMPLE 2:   Our neighbor owns an AKC-registered dog, *which* howls dur-
   ing the early morning hours.
   (*Which* refers to the non-human animal *dog*.)

c. *That* also refers to things or non-human animals, but it should not be used
   when the adjective clause is set off with commas.

   EXAMPLE 1:   This tree, *which* [*not that*] stands taller than any others nearby,
   provides shade for both of our yards.
   EXAMPLE 2:   Our neighbor owns the dog *that* howls during the early morning hours.

☞   Hint 2: Do not use <u>what</u> to start an adjective clause.

   EXAMPLE: Incorrect: The car *what* is painted blue is my mother's car.
   Correct: The car *that* is painted blue is my mother's car.
   Correct: The car, *which* is painted blue, is my mother's.

☞   Hint 3: Be sure the adjective clause is placed next to the word it
modifies.

☞   Hint 4: See Chapter 9, Rule 4, for punctuation of nonrestrictive
adjective clauses.

PART 3: ADVERB CLAUSE

A. **Characteristics:**

1. The adverb clause will have a subject and a verb and will start with one of these
   words:

after	because	though
although	before	unless
as	even though	until
as if	if	when
as long as	in order that	whenever
as much as	provided that	where
as soon as	since	wherever
as though	so that	while
	than	

2. Other characteristics of the adverb clause are similar to those of noun clauses.

B. **Function:** The adverb clause functions just like a single-word adverb: it modifies verbs, adjectives, and other adverbs; and it tells *when, where, why, how, to what extent,* and *under what conditions.*

The following examples show how adverb clauses function.

EXAMPLE 1: *After he washed the car*, the sky clouded, threatening rain.
(Subject, *he*; verb, *washed*; tells *when* about the verb *clouded*.)

EXAMPLE 2: *Although the water was choppy*, we found skiing conditions excellent.
(Subject, *water*; verb, *was*; tells *under what conditions* about the verb *found*.)

EXAMPLE 3: The shoppers dashed inside *as the rain began*.
(Subject, *rain*; verb, *began*; tells *when* about the verb *dashed*.)

EXAMPLE 4: The puppy ate *as if he had been without food for days*.
(Subject, *he*; verb, *had been*; tells *how* about the verb *ate*.)

EXAMPLE 5: He spent money *as long as he had it*.
(Subject, *he*; verb, *had*; tells *when* about the verb *spent*.)

EXAMPLE 6: I worked *as much as he did*.
(Subject, *he*; verb, *did*; tells *to what extent* about the verb *worked*.)

EXAMPLE 7: *As soon as we could*, we donned swimsuits and headed for the pool.
(Subject, *we*; verb, *could*; tells *when* about the verb *donned*.)

EXAMPLE 8: He studied *as though his life depended upon it*.
(Subject, *life*; verb, *depended*; tells *how* or *to what extent* about the verb *studied*.)

EXAMPLE 9: *Because the flood waters receded slowly*, deep layers of mud were left behind.
(Subject, *waters*; verb, *receded*; tells *why* about the verb *were left*.)

EXAMPLE 10: Aunt Thelma left *before we could say good-bye*.
(Subject, *we*; verb, *could say*; tells *when* about the verb *left*.)

EXAMPLE 11: I was angry *even though I understood his error*.
(Subject, *I*; verb, *understood*; tells *under what conditions* about the predicate adjective *angry*.)

EXAMPLE 12: *If you fail to pay your taxes*, you will be penalized.
(Subject, *you*; verb, *fail*; tells *under what conditions* about the verb *will be penalized*.)

EXAMPLE 13: *In order that yesterday's filing would be completed*, Jane worked two hours' overtime.
(Subject, *filing*; verb, *would be completed*; tells *why* about the verb *worked*.)

EXAMPLE 14: The desk would fit in the room, *provided that it was pushed snugly against the wall*.
(Subject, *it*; verb, *was pushed*; tells *under what conditions* about the verb *would fit*.)

EXAMPLE 15: *Since yesterday's snow storm ended*, we felt little security in camping out for the remainder of the week.
(Subject, *storm*; verb, *ended*; tells *when* about the verb *felt*.)

EXAMPLE 16: Juan rewrote his paper *so that it would be letter-perfect*.
(Subject, *it*; verb, *would be*; tells *why* about the verb *rewrote*.)

EXAMPLE 17: Martin worked harder *than Bill did*.
(Subject, *Bill*; verb, *did*; tells *to what extent* about the adverb *harder*.)

EXAMPLE 18: *Though mosquitoes swarmed above us*, they did not attack us until after dark.
(Subject, *mosquitoes*; verb, *swarmed*; tells *under what conditions* about the verb *did attack*.)

EXAMPLE 19: *Unless we collapse from exhaustion first*, we plan to finish cleaning the fish within an hour.
(Subject, *we*; verb, *collapse*; tells *under what conditions* about the verb *plan*.)

EXAMPLE 20: *When I attend a wedding*, I almost always cry.
(Subject, *I*; verb, *attend*; tells *when* about the verb *cry*.)

EXAMPLE 21: Our dog barks and growls *whenever the meter reader comes into the yard*.
(Subject, *reader*; verb, *comes*; tells *when* about the compound verb *barks and growls*.)

EXAMPLE 22: *While the flagman dozed in the afternoon sun*, his assistant directed traffic.
(Subject, *flagman*; verb, *dozed*; tells *when* about the verb *directed*.)

⇨ **Warning A: Some adverb clauses have a missing—but implied—verb.**

EXAMPLE: The assistant instructor worked harder preparing for the class *than I*.
(Adverb clause: *than I* [did])

⇨ **Warning B: Some adverb clauses have a missing—but implied—subject.**

EXAMPLE 1: *While driving to St. Louis*, he decided to travel on roads other than interstate highways.
(Adverb clause: *while* [he was] *driving to St. Louis*)

EXAMPLE 2: *When putting up a tent*, she always gets tangled in the ropes.
(Adverb clause: *when* [she is] *putting up a tent*)

☞ **Hint: Be sure that you do not say something ridiculous—even unintentionally—when there are implied subjects.**

EXAMPLE: Ridiculous: When putting up a tent, the ropes often get in the way.
(Since the subject is implied, the reader may think you intend *ropes* to be the subject! Ropes are not very good at putting up tents!)

Improved: When putting up a tent, you must keep the ropes untangled.
(Adverb clause: *when* [you are] *putting up a tent*)

⇨   Warning C: Do not confuse adverb clauses with prepositional phrases.

EXAMPLE 1:   *After dinner,* I took a nap.
                (*After* plus the noun *dinner* makes a prepositional phrase.)

                Compare that with the following:

EXAMPLE 2:   *After we ate dinner,* I took a nap.
                (*After* and a subject and a verb make an adverb clause.)

EXAMPLE 3:   I have slept *since one o'clock.*
                (*Since* and a noun make a prepositional phrase.)

                Compare that with the following:

EXAMPLE 4:   I have slept *since I came home from work.*
                (*Since* and a subject and verb make an adverb clause.)

✎   Remember: A clause must have a subject and a verb. A phrase does not.

☞   Hint: See Chapter 9, Rule 5, for punctuation of adverb clauses.

PRACTICE

Exercise 1

Directions: Work through the following sentences to find all the noun, adjective, and adverb clauses. Identify the function of each clause. Answers are printed after the sentences, but see if you really understand these clauses before you check. And read carefully. Many sentences have more than one dependent clause!

1. His new car, which was a four-cylinder model, gave him good gas mileage.

2. After the airplane engine was overhauled, the mechanic who had done most of the work pronounced the engine in good shape.

3. Honey bees, industrious creatures that they are, usually work themselves to death after six weeks of gathering honey.

4. Because the July heat was oppressive, the two hikers rested whenever they had the opportunity.

5. Whoever discovered that cooking dried corn in lye water makes hominy aided dietetic variety.

6. The dulcimer, which makes mandolin-like music, is not readily available in most music stores.

7. Because rip-rap rock is quite large, whoever works with it will be exhausted after he handles the first ton or so.

8. Whichever tree limbs are to be pruned should be clearly marked so that no one cuts off the wrong ones.

9. Whoever owns those Chinese geese that make such raucous noises must not be able to hear them when they create such a commotion that it awakens the entire neighborhood.

10. As the wind freshened, we anticipated a storm.

Exercise 1—Answers

1. *Which was a four-cylinder model* is an adjective clause that tells *which* about the noun *car*.

2. *After the airplane engine was overhauled* is an adverb clause that tells *when* about the verb *pronounced*. *Who had done most of the work* is an adjective clause that tells *which* about the noun *mechanic*.

3. *That they are* is an adjective clause that tells *what kind* about the noun *creatures*. *After* begins a prepositional phrase, not an adverb clause.

4. *Because the July heat was oppressive* is an adverb clause that tells *why* about the verb *rested*. *Whenever they had the opportunity* is an adverb clause that tells *when* about the verb *rested*.

5. *Whoever discovered that cooking dried corn in lye water makes hominy* is a noun clause that is the subject of the sentence. *That cooking dried corn in lye water makes hominy* is also a noun clause that is the object of the verb *discovered*. (So you have a clause within a clause. Fancy!)

6. *Which makes mandolin-like music* is an adjective clause that tells *what kind* about the noun *dulcimer*.

84

7. *Because rip-rap rock is quite large* is an adverb clause that tells *why* about the verb *will be exhausted. Whoever works with it* is a noun clause that is the subject of the main verb *will be exhausted. After he handles the first ton or so* is an adverb clause that tells *when* about the verb *will be exhausted.* (Did you find all three?)

8. *Whichever tree limbs are to be pruned* is a noun clause that is the subject of the sentence. *So that no one cuts off the wrong ones* is an adverb clause that tells *why* about the verb *should be marked.*

9. *Whoever owns those Chinese geese that make such raucous noises* is a noun clause that is subject of the sentence. *That make such raucous noises* is an adjective clause that tells *which* about the noun *geese.* (So you have a clause within a clause again!) *When they create such a commotion that it awakens the entire neighborhood* is an adverb clause that tells *when* about the infinitive *to hear. That it awakens the entire neighborhood* is an adjective clause within the adverb clause that tells *what kind* about the noun *commotion.* (All three kinds of clauses in one sentence!)

10. *As the wind freshened* is an adverb clause that tells *when* about the verb *anticipated.*

Exercise 2

Directions: The selection below includes both phrases and clauses. Identify each verbal phrase as a gerund, infinitive, or participle. Identify each noun, adjective, or adverb clause.

(1) Painting the kitchen turned out to be a real chore. (2) The problems all began when we discovered that the paint was semigloss instead of flat. (3) Although the semigloss goes on smoothly, we knew from experience that it would show the defects in the plaster, now crumbling from age. (4) We planned to patch the plaster before painting the walls; but with semigloss paint, the patches show. (5) Flat paint, on the other hand, tends to camouflage most of whatever shows. (6) Since we had painted the ceiling and one wall before we discovered our error, we were faced with a decision. (7) Should we buy more paint to repaint what we had already completed and add to both the expense and the work? (8) Or should we just finish the job and let the defects show?

Exercise 2—Answers

Sentence 1:

painting the kitchen (gerund phrase, subject); *to be . . . chore* (infinitive phrase, adverb modifying verb *turned out*)

Sentence 2:

when we discovered . . . instead of flat (adverb clause, modifying verb *began*); *that . . . paint . . . flat* (noun clause, direct object of verb *discovered*)

Sentence 3:

although . . . goes on smoothly (adverb clause, modifying verb *knew*); *that . . . would show . . . plaster . . . crumbling from age* (noun clause, direct object of verb *knew*); *now . . . age* (participial phrase, adjective modifying noun *plaster*)

Sentence 4:

to patch . . . the walls (infinitive phrase, direct object of verb *planning*); *painting . . . walls* (gerund phrase, object of preposition *before*)

Sentence 5:

whatever shows (noun clause, object of preposition *of*)

Sentence 6:

since we . . . painted . . . our error (adverb clause, modifying verb *were faced*); *before . . . error* (adverb clause, modifying verb *had painted*)

Sentence 7:

to repaint . . . already completed (infinitive phrase, adjective modifying noun *paint*); *what . . . already completed* (noun clause, direct object of *repaint*)

Sentence 8:

(none)

IV
PUNCTUATION

9

COMMAS

Now that you have a command of the fundamentals of grammar and the basic principles of usage, you are ready to punctuate. In an effort to simplify the many rules for using commas, this chapter condenses the rules to seven. These seven rules will solve ninety-nine percent of your problems.

 Remember: If there is no rule to indicate the need for a comma, do not use one. It is just as wrong to use unnecessary commas as it is to leave them out.

RULES

RULE 1: Use a comma to separate items in a series. A series is made up of three or more items. A series can be made up of nouns, verbs, modifiers, or phrases.

> EXAMPLES: —Series of *nouns: Dogs,* trapeze *artists,* and *clowns* all tumbled down the aisle together.
> —Series of *verbs:* The old truck *coughed, lurched,* and then *shuddered.*
> —Series of *modifiers:* Those hamburgers were *greasy, tasteless,* and *small.*
> —Series of *phrases:* We looked *under the rug, behind the pictures,* but not *inside the cabinet.*

☞ Hint A: To be safe and to avoid possible confusion, include the comma before the joining words like *and, or,* or *nor:* A, B, and C.

EXAMPLE: John, Tom, and Sue inherited $15,000.

☞ Hint B: If each item has a joining word after it, use no commas: A and B and C; A or B or C.

EXAMPLE 1: We swam and ate and slept for five days.
EXAMPLE 2: Milk or water or even ink would have tasted good to us.

☞ Hint C: Use no comma after the last item.

EXAMPLE: Maple, oak, and walnut trees provided dense shade.

RULE 2: Use a comma to separate coordinate adjectives. Coordinate adjectives are two or more adjectives that equally modify the same noun.

EXAMPLE: The low, heavy clouds threatened snow. (*Low* and *heavy* both modify clouds.)

To Test: You must be able to substitute *and* for the comma separating coordinate adjectives. Otherwise, you will use no comma.

EXAMPLE 1: A sleek, shiny new car sat in the driveway.
A sleek [and] shiny new car sat in the driveway.
But not: A sleek [and] shiny [and] new car sat in the driveway.

EXAMPLE 2: That pink flowering tree is especially pretty in the spring.
(*Pink* modifies *flowering* and *flowering* modifies *tree*. No comma. We cannot say *that pink and flowering tree.*)

Warning A: Use no comma if the word *and, or,* or *nor* actually appears between the two adjectives.

EXAMPLE: The long and arduous journey left the explorer with many memories, both pleasant and unpleasant.

Warning B: Omit the comma before numbers and before adjectives of size, shape, and age.

EXAMPLE 1: Three tired hikers napped against the tree trunks. (No comma after *three;* it is a *number.*)

EXAMPLE 2: The huge old house stood alone on the hill. (No comma after *huge;* it is an adjective of *size*. And *old* is also an adjective of *age.*)

EXAMPLE 3: A dilapidated two-storied house stood next door. (No comma after *dilapidated* since *two-storied* is an adjective of *shape.*)

RULE 3: Use a comma to separate two complete sentences joined by a conjunction (*and, but, or, nor,* or *for,* and sometimes *yet* and *so*).

EXAMPLE 1: Joan walked to the shopping center, but she found the stores all closed.
(You will see that we have joined two sentences with the conjunction *but: Joan walked to the shopping center. She found the stores all closed.* As you join the two sentences with *but,* replace the period with a comma so that you put the comma at the end of the first sentence.)

Compare that example with this one:

EXAMPLE 2: Joan walked to the shopping center and found that the stores were closed.
(Notice that you need no comma here since there are not two complete sentences—the verb is merely compound.)

Remember: With this rule, think of a comma plus a conjunction like *and, but, or, nor,* or *for* as being equal to a period. If you could not put in a period instead of the comma and conjunction, you do not have two sentences. Think of the rule this way:

$$, + \begin{Bmatrix} and \\ but \\ or \\ nor \\ for \end{Bmatrix} = .$$

▷ Warning: Be sure you have a complete sentence both before and after the conjunctions *and, but, or, nor,* or *for* before you put in a comma. Try substituting the period for the comma and conjunction to see if you have two sentences.

EXAMPLE 1: The calculator needed new batteries, but it seemed to be functioning accurately.

Two complete sentences:
—The calculator needed new batteries.
—It seemed to be functioning accurately.

(Two complete sentences are joined with a comma and a conjunction.)

EXAMPLE 2: The calculator needed new batteries but seemed to be functioning accurately.

One complete sentence:
—The calculator needed new batteries.
— . . . seemed to be functioning accurately.

(Since the second group of words is not a sentence, we do *not* use a comma and conjunction. We could *not* substitute with a period.)

RULE 4: Set off nonrestrictive verbal phrases or adjective clauses with commas.

A. *Set off* implies *two* commas—one before and one after—unless the phrase or clause is at the end of the sentence.
B. *Nonrestrictive* means "not essential" or "not needed to limit the noun."
C. A verbal phrase is a word group that begins with an infinitive or participle (see Chapter 7).
D. An adjective clause is a word group that has a subject and verb and starts with *who, whose, whom, which,* or *that* (see Chapter 8, Part 2, Adjective Clauses).

EXAMPLE 1: The brick house that was built across the street is for sale, but the brick house that was built next door is already sold.
(The adjective clauses *that was built across the street* and *that was built next door* are restrictive; that is, they are *necessary* to limit the noun they modify: *house.* Notice that if we read the sentence without the clauses, the sentence would not make much sense: The brick house is for sale, but the brick house is already sold.)

EXAMPLE 2: My sporty red Fiat, which my father gave me, is no longer in operating condition.
(The clause *which my father gave me* is not needed to limit *my sporty red Fiat.* I have only one! So the information in the clause is added information.)

☞ Hint: Think of added information as being a "by the way" idea: *By the way, my father gave me the Fiat.* By setting that information off with commas, you are saying that the "by the way" idea can be dropped out:

My sporty red Fiat
which [*by the way*] my father gave me
is no longer in operating condition.
(Think of the commas as arrows showing that the idea can be dropped without affecting the meaning of the noun it modifies, Fiat.)

EXAMPLE 3: Mr. Tzachosky, just getting off the boat, is a military agent.
(*Just getting off the boat* is a nonrestrictive—that is, nonessential—participial phrase. It is not needed to limit all Mr. Tzachoskys to just one. There is just one about whom the reader knows. The commas indicate that *just getting off the boat* is "by the way" information that can be dropped out.)

RULE 5: Set off introductory elements with a comma. Obviously, introductory elements appear at the beginning of the sentence! There are three kinds of introductory elements:

A. Introductory single words

EXAMPLES: *Yes,* I'm going to the game.
Oh, did you mean that?
Kathy, please open the door.

B. Introductory prepositional phrases of four or more words

EXAMPLE 1: *Behind the door of the closet,* we found the kitten asleep.
(Use the comma after this prepositional phrase. It has six words.)
EXAMPLE 2: *Around the corner* we ran into old friends.
(No comma is necessary after a prepositional phrase of only three words.)

C. Introductory verbal modifiers (see Chapter 7)

EXAMPLE 1: *Walking home from work,* he spotted two new species of birds in the neighborhood.
(Introductory participial phrase modifying *he*)
EXAMPLE 2: *To catch an early bus,* he left home fifteen minutes ahead of schedule.
(Introductory infinitive phrase modifying *he*)

⇨ Warning: If you use a comma, be sure the verbal is a *modifier*, not a subject.

EXAMPLE 1: Walking home from work is his usual form of exercise.
(Use no comma after *work* since *walking home from work* is the subject of the sentence.)
EXAMPLE 2: To catch an early bus was his daily goal.
(Use no comma after *bus* since *to catch an early bus* is the subject of the sentence.)

D. Introductory adverb clause (see Chapter 8, Part 3, Adverb Clauses)

EXAMPLE 1: *After we left,* the rain began.
(Subject, *we;* verb, *left;* tells *when* about *began.*)
EXAMPLE 2: *Because we all had eaten too much,* most of us fell asleep.
(Subject, *we;* verb, *had eaten;* tells *why* about *fell.*)
EXAMPLE 3: *If you know the answer,* don't tell!
(Subject, *you;* verb, *know;* tells *under what condition* about *tell.*)

NOTE: Unlike the limit of four words before using a comma after the introductory prepositional phrase (see Rule 5), there is no limit regarding adverb clauses.

EXAMPLE: *If you can,* call me about noon.
(Comma after only three words; it is an introductory adverb clause!)

RULE 6: Use Commas to set off interrupters. Interrupters come in the middle of the sentence and interrupt its natural flow. There are three kinds of interrupters.

A. Appositives (An appositive is a noun with its modifiers that renames another noun.)

EXAMPLE: Thornton Kleug, *a local author of some acclaim,* spoke at the Elks meeting.
(*A local author of some acclaim* is a noun, along with modifiers, that renames *Thornton Kleug.*)

NOTE: When an appositive appears at the end of the sentence, you will, of course, have only one comma.

B. Words of direct address (*Direct address* refers to speaking directly to someone.)

EXAMPLE 1: Will you, *John,* please close the door.
EXAMPLE 2: May I, *friends and neighbors,* ask your support?

☞ Hint: Compare these examples with Rule 5, Part A. If the noun of direct address comes at the beginning, you may think of it as introductory (requiring only one comma). If the noun of direct address comes in the middle of the sentence—interrupts the sentence—then you need a comma both before and after to set it off. If the noun of direct address comes at the end of the sentence, you will have only one comma.

C. Parenthetical expressions
The following are typical—but not all—parenthetical expressions:

of course	in fact	moreover
in the meantime	I believe	consequently
on the other hand	I hope	for example
therefore	I think	nevertheless
however	indeed	he said

EXAMPLE 1:   Our practice books, *on the other hand*, are more thorough than the preparation books.

EXAMPLE 2:   That so-called breeze, *as a matter of fact*, is more like a gale.

EXAMPLE 3:   "We will," John said, "complete the work as planned."

NOTE: Dozens of other interrupting phrases like *he explained, he yelled, he whispered* are set off by commas when they interrupt, precede, or follow direct quotations. See Chapter 11, Part 4, for a discussion of direct quotations.

➪   Warning: Sometimes these parenthetical expressions are used to join two sentences together. Then commas are not sufficient. See Chapter 10.

RULE 7:   Use commas to set off dates and states.

EXAMPLE 1:

Date:	January 5, 1935
Month and year:	January 1935
	(no comma needed)
Sentence:	January 5, 1935, was the date of her birth.
	(two commas needed)

EXAMPLE 2:

City and state:	Louisville, Kentucky
Sentence:	Louisville, Kentucky, is her home.
	(two commas needed)

Summary for Using Commas

Rule 1:   Series

Rule 2:   Coordinate adjectives
(except size, shape, age, and numbers)

Rule 3:   Two sentences with conjunction
_____, and _____.

Rule 4:   Nonrestrictive
A. Adjective clause
B. Verbal phrase

Rule 5:   Introductory
A. Single words
B. Prepositional phrase of four or more words
C. Verbal modifier
D. Adverb clause

Rule 6:   Interrupters
A. Appositive
B. Direct address
C. Parenthetical expressions

Rule 7:   Dates and states

PRACTICE

Exercise 1

Directions: Add commas where necessary to the following passage. Check your answers with those below and review the rules as necessary.

(1) Soon after the storm hit streets and roads were flooded. (2) At the same time high winds made dangerous missiles of ordinary objects. (3) Tree limbs downed wires trash cans and other debris created further dangerous driving conditions. (4) Together the flooding high winds and debris caused city officials to ask residents to stay off the streets. (5) The dangerous conditions continued throughout most of the night but residents gingerly picked their way to work and school the next morning.

Exercise 1—Answers

Sentence 1:

hit, (Rule 5, Part D)

Sentence 2:

time, (Rule 5, Part B)

Sentence 3:

limbs, wires, cans, (Rule 1)

Sentence 4:

Together, (Rule 5, Part A); flooding, winds, (Rule 1)

Sentence 5:

night, (Rule 3)

A complete review of punctuation appears at the end of Chapter 11.

10
SEMICOLONS AND COLONS

In an effort to make punctuation as plain and simple as possible, this chapter gives three rules for using semicolons and three rules for using colons.

PART 1: SEMICOLONS

There are three basic reasons for using semicolons:

A. Use a semicolon to join two sentences when there is *no* coordinating conjunction like *and, or, nor, for*, and sometimes *yet* and *so*. Think of this diagram to help you remember:

(sentence)	*, and*	_(sentence)_
	OR	
(sentence)	**;**	_(sentence)_

EXAMPLE: Sue Ellen missed the bus, *so* she was late for her appointment.
Sue Ellen missed the bus; she was late for her appointment.

➪ Warning: When sentences are joined by a conjunctive adverb, such as *consequently, therefore, nevertheless, moreover,* or *however,* you need not only a semicolon *before* but also a comma *after* the conjunctive adverb. (See Rule 6 in Chapter 9.)

EXAMPLE: Sue Ellen missed the bus; *therefore,* she was late for her appointment.

Think of these diagrams when joining two sentences:

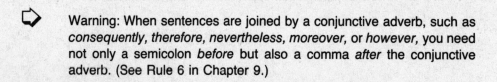

(sentence)	*, and*	_(sentence)_
(sentence)	**;**	_(sentence)_
(sentence)	**;** *therefore,*	_(sentence)_

☞ Hint: To be joined with a semicolon, the ideas in the two sentences should be closely related.

EXAMPLE: George and his father fished steadily for six hours; their efforts were futile.

96

B. Use a semicolon to separate two sentences that are joined by a conjunction but that have other commas within either of the two sentences.
Think of the following diagram to clarify the rule: (Each line represents a complete sentence.)

```
_____    , and   _____ .
_____ ,    ; and   _____ .
_____    ; and   _____ , _ .
_____ ,      ; and   _____ , _ .
```

EXAMPLE 1:   The teachers were eager to go home, *but* they took with them all the papers to be graded for the next week.
(The comma and conjunction *but* are sufficient to separate the two sentences.)

EXAMPLE 2:   When school was dismissed Friday, the teachers were eager to go home; *but* they took with them all the papers to be graded for the next week.
(Now we have a comma in the first sentence—an introductory element, Rule 5—so the comma and conjunction *but* are no longer sufficient. The comma in front of *but* becomes a semicolon.)

C. Use a semicolon to separate items in a series if there are commas within the items.

EXAMPLE 1:   Mr. Brown had baked a cake; Miss Johnson, an apple pie; Mrs. Rolfe, a pan of biscuits.
(There are three items in the series:

1. Mr. Brown had baked a cake
2. Miss Johnson, an apple pie
3. Mrs. Rolfe, a pan of biscuits

Since there are commas within the items themselves, the items must be separated from each other with semicolons.)

EXAMPLE 2:   The prize winners came from Waukegan, Illinois; Denton, Texas; and Hillside, New York.
(The three items in the series are as follows:

1. Waukegan, Illinois
2. Denton, Texas
3. Hillside, New York

Since there are commas within the items, the items must be separated with semicolons.)

PART 2: COLONS

There are three reasons for using a colon:

A. Use a colon for certain conventional items.

1. Giving the time

   EXAMPLE: 3:15 PM

2. Separating chapter from verse in Bible references

   EXAMPLE: John 3:16

3. Separating volume from page in bibliography references

EXAMPLE: Reader's Digest 146:72 (The volume is 146 and the page is 72.)

4. Giving a salutation in a business letter

EXAMPLE: Dear Sir:

B.   Use a colon to introduce a formal list.

EXAMPLE: We bought the following items: ground beef, hamburger buns, potato chips, and cokes.

☞   Hint: The words *following* or *as follows* or *these* are often clue words.

⇨   Warning: Do *not* use a colon after a preposition or after a linking verb.

✎   Remember: Prepositions are followed by objects, and linking verbs are followed by predicate words. Sometimes, these objects and predicate words are compound, or even in a series. But *do not* separate the preposition from its object or the linking verb from its predicate word with *any* kind of punctuation.

EXAMPLE 1:   The days on which applications will be accepted are Tuesday, Wednesday, and Thursday. (Do not use a colon after the linking verb *are*.)

EXAMPLE 2:   The days on which applications will be accepted are the following: Tuesday, Wednesday, and Thursday.
(Use a colon after the clue word *following* to introduce a list.)

EXAMPLE 3:   Applications will be accepted on these dates: June 6, 7, and 8.
(Use a colon after the clue word *these* to introduce a list.)

☞   Hint: Sometimes a complete thought can end in a preposition or linking verb. In that case—and only in that case—a colon can follow a preposition or linking verb.

EXAMPLE 1:   I know what the answers are: A, B, B, A.
(A complete thought precedes the linking verb.)

EXAMPLE 2:   I know what it is made of: rubber and wood.
(A complete thought precedes the preposition.)

The reason for these colons in the two above examples is explained in the following rule:

C.   Use a colon to mean "summary follows" or "explanation follows." The explanation is usually a complete sentence, and the summary is usually a series of words or phrases.

EXAMPLE 1:   He was limping badly: he had burned his foot when he spilled the boiling water.
(The second sentence explains the first.)

EXAMPLE 2:   The theater boasted a successful season: excellent ticket sales, increased revenue, and favorable critics' reviews.
(The items after the colon summarize the conditions involved in a successful season.)

Summary for Using Semicolons and Colons

I. Semicolons

    A. Joining sentences with no conjunction

        _____ ; _____ .

        _____ ; *therefore,* _____ .

    B. Separating two sentences with conjunction and other commas

        ____ , ____ ; *and* _____

        _____ ; *and* ____ , ____

        ____ , ____ ; *and* ____ , ____

    C. Separating items in a series if commas appear within the items

II. Colons

    A. Conventional items

    B. List (except after prepositions or linking verbs)

    C. "Summary or explanation follows"

PRACTICE

Exercise 1

Directions: The following selection may need commas, semicolons, and colons. Add where necessary, and then check your answers below.

(1) Whenever I'm late for anything I can always look back and see that I have not planned carefully. (2) If I could just learn to look at the clock work backwards from the appointed day or time and plan a schedule accordingly I could avoid these frustrating situations. (3) Remembering to do that however isn't easy for me. (4) Even when I do remember to make a schedule I find it isn't always realistic and then finding myself late again I feel even more frustrated. (5) I need a magic clock in my brain!

Exercise 1—Answers

Sentence 1:

anything, (Rule 5, Part D, page 93)

Sentence 2:

clock, time, (Rule 1, page 89); accordingly, (Rule 5, Part C, page 92)

Sentence 3:

that, however, (Rule 6, Part C, pages 93–94)

Sentence 4:

schedule, (Rule 5, Part D, page 93); realistic; (Part B, page 97); then, again, (Rule 6, Part C, pages 93–94)

Sentence 5:

(none)

A complete review of punctuation appears at the end of Chapter 11.

11

OTHER PUNCTUATION

Since most other marks of punctuation are relatively simple, only the bare minimum is included here.

PART 1: END MARKS

A. Period

1. Use a period at the end of a statement.
2. Use a period for an abbreviation.

☞ Hint: Most governmental agency and international organization abbreviations are *not* followed with periods.

EXAMPLES: Interstate Commerce Commission = ICC
United Nations = UN

B. Exclamation Point

Use an exclamation point at the end of an exclamatory sentence or expression.

EXAMPLE: What a game*!*

C. Question Mark

1. Use a question mark to ask a question.

EXAMPLE: Where is the nearest gas station?

2. Do not use a question mark after an indirect question.

EXAMPLE: I wonder where the nearest gas station is.

3. It is not usually necessary to use a question mark after a polite command.

EXAMPLE: Mary, will you please come here.

PART 2: APOSTROPHES

A. Use the apostrophe to show possession.

1. Use the following steps to formulate the possessive:

   a. Write the word to be made possessive in a prepositional phrase.

EXAMPLE 1:	That *cats* ears are pointed.
	The ears *of that cat* are pointed.
EXAMPLE 2:	All the team *members* shoes are wet.
	The shoes of *all the team members* are wet.
EXAMPLE 3:	He earned two *weeks* pay.
	He earned the pay *of two weeks*.
EXAMPLE 4:	An *hours* time is all I can spare.
	The time *of an hour* is all I can spare.

   b. Add the apostrophe to the object of the preposition and eliminate the other words.

   EXAMPLES: . . .cat'
   . . .members'
   . . .weeks'
   . . .hour'

   c. If the word does not end in an -*s*, add it.

   EXAMPLES:

cat'	cat's	—The *cat's* ears are pointed.
members'	(no change)	—All the team *members'* shoes are wet
weeks'	(no change)	—He earned two *weeks'* pay.
hour'	hour's	—An *hour's* time is all I can spare.

2. Some peculiar situations sometimes result when forming possessives.

   a. If you add an apostrophe to a *singular* word that ends in -*s* and that is just one syllable, then you *will* add another -*s*.

   EXAMPLES: —Charles's
   (*Charles* is singular and only one syllable, so you need the extra -*s*.)

   —waitress'
   (*Waitress* is singular but two syllables, so you do *not* add an extra -*s*.)

   b. Compound words are usually made plural at the end of the first word and always made possessive at the end of the second.

   EXAMPLES: sister-in-law
   two sisters-in-law (plural)
   sister-in-law's car (possessive)
   two sisters-in-law's cars (plural possessive)

   c. Sometimes two people are involved in ownership.

     1) If two people own something together, the second word shows the ownership.

       EXAMPLE: Mother and Dad's house
               (jointly owned)

     2) If two people own something separately, *both* words show ownership.

       EXAMPLE: Eisenhower's and Kennedy's administrations
               (Each had his own administration.)

B. Use apostrophes to show omissions.

    EXAMPLES: cannot—can't
               crash of 1929—crash of '29

C. Use apostrophes to show plurals of letters, signs, numbers, and words referred to as words.

    EXAMPLES: Avoid *you's* in formal writing.   } See also Part 3
               Be sure to cross your *t's*   Italics, Section C

PART 3: ITALICS

(Italics are indicated by underlining in handwritten or typewritten work.)

A. Use italics for foreign words.

    EXAMPLE: He graduated *summa cum laude*.

B. Use italics for titles of long works like books, periodicals, and movies. (Compare with Part 4, Quotation Marks, Section B.)

    EXAMPLE: The latest issue of *US News and World Report* is lying on the sofa.

C. Use italics for letters or words referred to as such.

    EXAMPLES: The *i* looked like an *e*.
              Too many *and's* appeared in the paragraph.
              (See also Part 2, Apostrophes, Section C.)

PART 4: QUOTATION MARKS

A. Use quotation marks to set off someone's direct words.

    EXAMPLE 1: He said, "I watched the moon rise late last night."
              (His exact words are in quotation marks.)
    EXAMPLE 2: He said that he watched the moon rise late last night.
              (No quotation marks needed. His direct words are not given.)

B. Use quotation marks around titles of smaller works.

EXAMPLE: "How to Retire Early" appeared in last month's issue of *Business Week*.

Compare this rule with Part 3, Italics, Section B. Then, think in terms of the following summary:

Italics	*Quotation Marks*
name of magazine	magazine article
name of book	chapter in book
name of newspaper	newspaper article
name of musical	individual song

C. Use quotation marks around the definition of a word.

EXAMPLE: *Austere* means "serious, stern." (Compare with Part 3, Italics, Section C. The word *austere* is italicized since it is referred to as a word, but the definition of that word goes in quotation marks.)

PART 5: MULTIPLE PUNCTUATION MARKS

Now let us consider some general rules for the placement of punctuation marks when more than one mark is needed after a single word.

RULE 1: Never use two end marks of punctuation together.

RULE 2: Never use a comma with an end mark.

RULE 3: When using quotation marks,
—put periods and commas *inside* closing quotation marks.

EXAMPLES: ."
,"
Not ",
".

—put question marks and exclamation marks either inside or outside closing quotation marks, depending on which part of the sentence is the question or exclamation.

EXAMPLE 1: The skier asked, "Is the chair lift operating yet?"
(The question mark goes with the question *Is the chair lift operating yet.*)

EXAMPLE 2: Did the skier say, "I'm planning to ski the west slope"?
(The whole sentence, not the quotation, is the question. The question mark goes *after* the quotation marks.)

—put semicolons and colons outside closing quotation marks.

EXAMPLE: The man threatened, "I won't help you"; however, I didn't believe him.

PRACTICE

Exercise 1

Directions: You now have the basics of punctuation! Using the summaries at the ends of Chapters 9 and 10 to refresh your memory, apply what you have learned in these last three chapters to complete the following punctuation review. When you have punctuated these sentences as accurately as you can, check your answers with those that follow the sentences. Rule and section numbers are given with the answers so that you can review those items that may still be causing you some difficulty.

1. After we watched the martins diving acrobatics for nearly an hour Delbert the local ornithologist explained how they feed on insects caught in midair.

2. The following pear trees were grouped together in the orchard Bartlett Golden Delicious and his favorite Starking Delicious.

3. Gentlemen may I ask your support in Barbara and Gerald endeavor in working with The Daily News he said.

4. My editor-in-chief attitude which was indeed not at all difficult to accept reflected his superior education and extensive experience.

5. Changing flat tires adjusting carburetors and checking the timing were part of his daily work but he resented doing that same work at home for nonpaying relatives.

6. Yes many people believe that Boonville Indiana located in the southern tip of the state was named after Daniel Boone.

7. Ruffled by the wind the tall golden wheat makes a cool and restful summer scene except to the farmer who finds harvesting the wheat and baling the straw hot itchy work.

8. The elevated highway described in the pamphlet Getting Around Town provided quick transportation around the city but gaining access to it was a real puzzle.

9. In the left-hand corner of the top drawer you will find my dear a special surprise package for you.

10. Studying horoscopes interests her for a special reason she believes her own life is guided by the sign of Capricorn.

11. Talking in front of his peers gave him practice talking in front of strangers became easier.

12. Those committee members who worked most diligently at this assignment will be financially rewarded and recognized at the national meeting.

Exercise 1—Answers

1. After we watched the martins' diving acrobatics for nearly an hour, Delbert, the local ornithologist, explained how they feed on insects caught in midair.
   martins' (Chapter 11, Part 2, Section A)
   hour, (Chapter 9, Rule 5, Part D)
   Delbert, ornithologist, (Chapter 9, Rule 6, Part A)

2. The following pear trees were grouped together in the orchard: Bartlett; Golden Delicious; and his favorite, Starking Delicious.
   orchard: (Chapter 10, Part 2, Section B or C)
   Bartlett; (Chapter 10, Part 1, Section C)

Delicious; (Chapter 10, Part 1, Section C)
favorite, (Chapter 9, Rule 6, Part A)

3. "Gentlemen, may I ask your support in Barbara and Gerald's endeavor in working with *The Daily News*," he said.
   "Gentlemen (Chapter 11, Part 4, Section A)
   Gentlemen, (Chapter 9, Rule 5, Part A)
   Barbara and Gerald's (Chapter 11, Part 2, Section A, 2, c)
   The Daily News (Chapter 11, Part 3, Section B)
   News, (Chapter 9, Rule 6, Part C. Note: a question mark is not necessary as internal punctuation because this is a polite request, not a question.)
   News," (Chapter 11, Part 4, Section A)

4. My editor-in-chief's attitude, which was, indeed, not at all difficult to accept, reflected his superior education and extensive experience.
   editor-in-chief's (Chapter 11, Part 2, Section A, 2, b)
   attitude, (Chapter 9, Rule 4, Part A)
   was, indeed, (Chapter 9, Rule 6, Part C)
   accept, (Chapter 9, Rule 4, Part A)

5. Changing flat tires, adjusting carburetors, and checking the timing were part of his daily work; but he resented doing that same work at home for nonpaying relatives.
   tires, carburetors, (Chapter 9, Rule 1)
   work; (Chapter 10, Part 1, Section B)

6. Yes, many people believe that Boonville, Indiana, located in the southern tip of the state, was named after Daniel Boone.
   Yes, (Chapter 9, Rule 5, Part A)
   Boonville, (Chapter 9, Rule 7)
   Indiana, (Chapter 9, Rule 7 or Rule 4, Part B)
   state, (Chapter 9, Rule 4, Part B)

7. Ruffled by the wind, the tall, golden wheat makes a cool and restful summer scene except to the farmer, who finds harvesting the wheat and baling the straw hot, itchy work.
   wind, (Chapter 9, Rule 5, Part C)
   tall, (Chapter 9, Rule 2)
   farmer, (Chapter 9, Rule 4, Part A)
   hot, (Chapter 9, Rule 2)

8. The elevated highway described in the pamphlet "Getting Around Town" provided quick transportation around the city, but gaining access to it was a real puzzle.
   "Getting Around Town" (Chapter 11, Part 4, Section B)
   city, (Chapter 9, Rule 3)

9. In the left-hand corner of the top drawer, you will find, my dear, a special surprise package for you.
   drawer, (Chapter 9, Rule 5, Part B)
   find, dear, (Chapter 9, Rule 6, Part B)

10. Studying horoscopes interests her for a special reason: she believes her own life is guided by the sign of Capricorn.
    reason: (Chapter 10, Part 2, Section C)

11. Talking in front of his peers gave him practice; talking in front of strangers became easier.
    practice; (Chapter 10, Part 1, Section A)

12. No further punctuation needed

12

CAPITALIZATION

The following rules for capitalization cover most common needs.

RULE 1: Capitalize the first word in sentences.

> EXAMPLE: The news anchor reported the disputes.

☞ Hint: Remember to capitalize the first word of someone else's sentence in a quotation. (See Chapter 11, Part 4, for rules about quotation marks.)

> EXAMPLE: Marion asked, "Have you paid the utility bill?"
> ("Have" is the first word of Marion's quoted sentence.)

➪ Warning: Do *not* capitalize the first word of a continuing quotation.

> EXAMPLE: "Have you paid the utility bill," Marion asked, "or shall I pay it?"
> ("Or" is *not* capitalized since it continues the quotation.)

RULE 2: Capitalize titles.

Titles of people: Dr. Karla Jeffers, Mrs. Todd, President Bush, Senator Lugar, Uncle Bob, Grandmother Dixon, Father

➪ Warning: Do *not* capitalize common nouns.

> EXAMPLE: Mother, but my mother; Grandmother Dixon, but his grandmother; Senator Lugar, but a senator.

➪ Warning: Do *not* capitalize titles that appear *after* names.

> EXAMPLE: Dr. Karla Jeffers, but Karla Jeffers the doctor.

Titles of Publications, Works of Art: "Stress in the Work Place," *Gone with the Wind*, *U.S. News and World Report*, the Mona Lisa.

NOTE: Book and magazine titles are italicized (underlined) and article and chapter titles are enclosed in quotation marks. See Chapter 11, Parts 3 and 4.

Warning: Do *not* capitalize *a*, *an*, and *the* or prepositions in titles *unless* they come at the beginning or end of the title.

EXAMPLE: *From Here to Eternity, The Comedy of Neil Simon*

RULE 3:   Capitalize proper names and words made from the proper names.

Names of days, months, holidays: Monday, February, Thanksgiving (but not seasons: spring, autumn)

Geographic names: Scott County, Miami, Alaska, Lake Michigan, Missouri River, Rocky Mountains, France, the Midwest, the South (but not midwestern or directions: north, south), Williams Street (but not street and not streets as in the corner of Williams and Main streets)

Business names: Ford Motor Company, Kleenex, Pepsi, Scotch tape

School names and subjects: Oakland City College, World Economics 202 (but not economics), Geography I (but not geography)

Religious names and pronouns: Trinity Lutheran Church, the Koran, God, His teachings, Buddha, Mennonite

Names of people and languages: Roman, Chinese, Vietnamese

Abbreviations of proper names: CST (Central Standard Time), NATO (North Atlantic Treaty Organization), FBI (Federal Bureau of Investigation)

RULE 4:   Capitalize the first word and all nouns in the salutation of a letter and the first word in the closing of a letter.

EXAMPLE: Dear Mr. Warner but My dear Miss Sarah; Fondly yours, Sincerely

PRACTICE

Exercise 1

Directions: Add capital letters where needed. Answers follow and refer you to specific rules.

1. the french delegation visited chicago, illinois, and stopped to shop at bloomingdale's.

2. please plan to arrive at 1412 wilmont street by 9:00 est if you want to meet senator johnston.

3. as ernest explained, "working late on the north side of town is okay from march through october, but the drive along riverview expressway is treacherous in winter."

4. since he hails from the west, professor stuart wears boots and hats reminiscent of john wayne movies.

5. a book called *jobs for everyone* gives good tips on how to make the most of one's skills.

6. Carlos mailed the check on saturday at the city post office, but by wednesday it still had not reached st. louis, missouri.

7. when my uncle harry met your uncle, they traded world war II stories about the south pacific.

8. at the corner of main and division streets stands a magazine store that always has copies of *usa today*.

9. are some of your chinese friends buddhists?

10. on new year's day we always eat cabbage since our polish family is superstitious.

Exercise 1—Answers

1. The (first word in sentence), French (nationality), Chicago, Illinois (geographic names), Bloomingdale's (business)

2. Please (first word in sentence), Wilmont Street (geographic name), EST (abbreviation of proper name: Eastern Standard Time), Senator Johnston (title of person)

3. As (first word in sentence), Ernest (proper name), Working (first word in quoted sentence), March, October, (months), Riverview Expressway (geographic name)

4. Since (first word in sentence), West (geographic region), Professor Stuart (title of person), John Wayne (proper name)

5. A (first word in sentence), *Jobs for Everyone* (book title)

6. Carlos (proper name and first word in sentence), Saturday, Wednesday (days of week), St. Louis, Missouri (geographic name)

7. When (first word in sentence), Uncle Harry (title), World War II (proper name), South Pacific (geographic area)

8. At (first word in sentence), Main, Division (geographic names), *USA Today* (title of newspaper)

9. Are (first word in sentence), Chinese (nationality), Buddhists (religious reference)

10. On (first word in sentence), New Year's Day (holiday), Polish (nationality)

13

COMMONLY CONFUSED WORDS

The following words are commonly confused. Be sure you know how to use them correctly.

accept, except

Accept means "to receive." It is always a verb. Example: He *accepted* the gift.

Except is most often a preposition. Example: I ate everything *except* the pie.
Except is sometimes a verb. Then it means "to leave out or omit." Example: The judge *excepted* the man from jury duty.

affect, effect

Affect is always a verb. It means "to influence" or "to bring about a change." Example: Will the weather *affect* your plans?

Effect is usually a noun. It means "result." Example: What *effect* will the pay raise have on you?
Effect can also be a verb. Then it means "to bring about" or "to accomplish." Example: The negotiator *effected* a compromise between the company and union officials.

all ready, already

All ready means "everything is ready." Example: The fabric, pattern, scissors, and pins are *all ready* for the seamstress.

Already is an adverb. It means "by or before a given time." Example: We were *already* late for dinner when we had the flat tire.

amount, number

Amount is used to refer to things we cannot count. Example: The *amount* of sugar he uses is unhealthy. (We cannot count sugar: 1 sugar, 2 sugars, etc.)

Number is used to talk about things we can count. Example: The number of cups of sugar in the recipe surprised me. (We can count cups of sugar: 1 cup, 2 cups, etc.)

between, among

Between is used to refer to two items. Example: Divide this pie *between* the two of you.

Among is used to refer to more than two items. Example: Can you choose from *among* the three dresses?

borrow, lend

Borrow means "to take or receive something" with the understanding that it will be returned. Example: He asked to *borrow* my lawn mower.

Lend means "to allow someone to use something" of yours. Example: Yes, I will *lend* him my lawn mower.

bring, take

Bring means "to carry or lead to where the speaker is." Example: Tiffanie will *bring* potato salad to our carry-in supper.

Take means "to carry or lead away from where the speaker is." Example: Tiffanie will *take* potato salad to the neighbor's carry-in supper.

capital, the Capitol

Capital refers to wealth. Example: I don't have the *capital* to finance a new car. *Capital* also refers to the seat of state government. Example: Frankfort is the *capital* of Kentucky.

Capitol (always with an uppercase C) refers to the building in Washington D.C. where the U.S. Congress meets. Example: While in our nation's capital, we toured the *Capitol*.

desert, desert, dessert

Desert (pronounced de sert') is a verb. It means "to leave." Example: How strange that the cat *deserted* her kittens.

Desert (pronounced des' ert) is a noun. It refers to dry, sandy regions. Example: The Mohave Desert has a mysterious beauty all its own.

Dessert refers to a sweet something eaten at the end of a meal. Example: Apple pie is Dad's favorite *dessert*.

different from

Say *different from*, not *different than*. Example: This paint surface is *different from* that one.

farther, further

Farther refers to physical distance. Example: How much *farther* is it to the next rest area?

Further means "in addition." Example: I needed *further* explanation in order to understand the problem.

fewer, less

Fewer, like *number*, refers to things we can count. Example: Use *fewer* cups of sugar when you make this recipe. (We can count cups: 1 cup, 2 cups, etc.)

Less, like *amount*, refers to things we cannot count. Example: Use *less* sugar than the recipe calls for. (We cannot count sugar: 1 sugar, 2 sugars, etc.)

had of, off of

Omit *of*. Examples: I *had* gone home by then. He fell *off* the bicycle.

hear, here

Hear is one of the five senses. (Note the word *ear* in *hear*.)
Example: Fred can *hear* water dripping somewhere.

Here refers to a place. (Note that its opposite, *there*, has the word *here* in it.)
Example: Put the book *here* on the table.

imply, infer

Imply means "to suggest a meaning" when you make a statement. Example: Did you *imply* that you don't like my dress?

Infer means "to draw meaning out of" what someone else says. Example: She *inferred* that I didn't like her dress, but she was wrong.

its, it's

Its is a possessive pronoun. Example: The dog lost *its* collar.

It's is a contraction for *it is*. The apostrophe shows the omission of the second *i*.
Example: *It's* (It is) really cold today.

whose, who's

Whose is a possessive pronoun. Example: *Whose* coat is this?

Who's is a contraction for *who is*. The apostrophe shows the omission of the *i*.
Example: *Who's* (Who is) going with me in my car?

learn, teach

Learn means "to gain knowledge." Example: Ned *learned* how to ski last summer.

Teach means "to give knowledge." Example: Carlton *taught* Ned to ski last summer.

lend, loan

Lend is a verb. (See *borrow, lend*.) Example: He *lent* me his lawn mower. (Do not say, "He *loaned* me his lawn mower.")

Loan is a noun. Example: The lawn mower was only a *loan*.

let, leave

Let means "to allow." Example: Please *let* me help you.

Leave means "to go away." Example: I'll *leave* in five minutes.

like, as

Like is a preposition and is followed by a noun. Example: He looks just *like* his brother.

As is an introductory word that is followed by a noun and a verb. Example: Gerald runs *as* I do.

loose, lose

Loose means "not tight." Example: The steering is *loose* in the old truck.

Lose means "to not know the whereabouts" of something. Example: I'm afraid I will *lose* this expensive ring.

of, have

Use *have*, not *of*, with *could*. Example: I *could have* called earlier.

principal, principle

Principal can be a noun or an adjective. As an adjective it means "main." Example: Protecting pedestrians is the *principal* reason for the law. As a noun it means "the main person in a school" or "a sum of money." Example: Mrs. Caston is the *principal* at Hinton High School. We invested a *principal* of $1000 in a savings certificate.

Principle is a noun and means "underlying rule." Example: We studied the *principles* of economics.

stationary, stationery

Stationary means "not moving." Example: He rides a *stationary* bicycle for exercise in the winter.

Stationery means "writing materials," especially paper. Example: I received a letter on the President's personal *stationery*.

their, there, they're

Their is a possessive pronoun. It shows ownership. Example: The men left *their* jackets in the car.

There is the opposite of *here* and refers to a place. (Notice that the word *there* is made up of the word *here* plus a *t*.) Example: Put your cola *there* on the coaster.

They're is a contraction for *they are*, and the apostrophe shows the missing *a*. Example: I'm sure *they're* (they are) home.

to, too, two

To is used with a noun or with a verb. Examples: Walter went *to* the races. (*to* followed by a noun) Do you want *to* eat lunch at 11:30? (*to* followed by a verb)

Too means "also" or "excessively." Examples: I'm driving. Are you driving *too*? That print is *too* small to read without my glasses.

Two means 2. Example: He reserved a table for *two*.

way, ways

Way is singular. Examples: San Francisco is a long *way* from New York. Your *way* is better than mine.

Ways is plural. Example: There are three *ways* to reach the industrial center.

weather, whether

Weather refers to climate. Example: This rainy *weather* should make the plants grow.

Whether shows a choice. Example: I don't know *whether* to apply for a different job or not.

your, you're

Your is a possessive pronoun. Example: Don't forget *your* tickets!

You're is a contraction for *you are*, and the apostrophe shows the missing *a*. Example: I hope *you're* (you are) staying for lunch.

14

GED PRACTICE FOR SECTIONS I TO IV

You have studied the fundamentals of the English language, elements of usage, phrases and clauses, and punctuation. What you need to understand now is how those kinds of things will appear on the GED test. You will *not* be asked to identify all of the parts of speech in a sentence or underline the phrases or identify the kinds of clauses. Rather, you will be asked to *apply* what you know about parts of speech, phrases and clauses, and usage to improve sentences or correct errors. The following sample will familiarize you with the GED approach. (You will find another sample in Chapter 25 that lets you practice what you will learn in Sections V to VII.)

The following sample includes directions. Work your way through the sample, and then study the answers that follow. You will find not only the correct answer listed but also a discussion of each of the other choices. By studying all of the responses, you can learn to think your way through the test. The more you understand about how to take the test, the more successful you will be. So practice carefully now!

SAMPLE PRACTICE TEST

Directions: Choose the *one best answer* to each item. Items 1 to 10 refer to the following paragraph.

(1) Between the controversies facing tax revenue planners is one over sales tax. (2) Some experts think we pay too much sales tax. (3) He believes instead that the value-added tax is more fair than a sales tax. (4) A value-added tax are those that tax each step of production. (5) For instance, a company that makes aluminum cans pays tax only on the value it's process puts in the cans. (6) Here's how it works. (7) Perhaps the sheet aluminum is worth $1.00 but the finished aluminum cans are worth $4.00. (8) After the process is finished the can maker pays tax only on the $3.00 value added to the product. (9) When the Beverage Company fills the $4.00 cans to make them worth $10.00, it pays tax on the $6.00 added value. (10) When you and I buy the canned beverage, we pay no tax. (11) Except, of course, indirectly through increased prices.

1. Sentence 1: Between the controversies facing tax revenue planners is one over sales tax.

   What correction should be made to the sentence?

   (1) Replace *is* with *are*.
   (2) Change *sales* to *sale's*.
   (3) Replace *between* with *among*.
   (4) Insert a comma after *planners*.
   (5) No correction is necessary.

2. Sentence 2: Some experts think we pay too much sales tax.

   What correction should be made to the sentence?

   (1) Replace *too much* with *too many*.
   (2) Change *sales* to *sale's*.
   (3) Insert a comma after *experts*.
   (4) Change *too* to *to*.
   (5) No correction is necessary.

3. Sentence 3: He believes instead that the value-added tax is more fair than a sales tax.

   What correction should be made to the sentence?

   (1) Change *he believes* to *they believe*.
   (2) Replace *more fair* with *more fairer*.
   (3) Insert a comma after *instead*.
   (4) Replace *is* with *are*.
   (5) No correction is necessary.

4. Sentence 4: A value-added tax are those that tax each step of production.

   What correction should be made to the sentence?

   (1) Change *that tax* to *that taxes*.
   (2) Replace *are those that tax* with *is one that taxes*.
   (3) Insert a comma after *value-added tax*.
   (4) Change *are* to *were*.
   (5) No correction is necessary.

5. Sentence 5: For instance, a company that makes aluminum cans pays tax only on the value it's process puts in the cans.

   What correction should be made to this sentence?

   (1) Change *it's* to *its*.
   (2) Omit the comma after *instance*.
   (3) Replace *pays* with *pay*.
   (4) Change *pays tax only* to *pays only tax*.
   (5) No correction is necessary.

6. Sentence 6: Here's how it works.

   What correction should be made to this sentence?

   (1) Change *it works* to *they work*.
   (2) Replace *Here's* with *Hear's*.
   (3) Change *Here's* to *Here are*.
   (4) Change the period to a colon.
   (5) No correction is necessary.

7. Sentence 7: Perhaps the sheet aluminum is <u>worth $1.00 but the finished</u> aluminum cans are worth $4.00.

   Which of the following is the best way to write the underlined portion of this sentence? If you think the original is the best way, choose option (1).

   (1) worth $1.00 but the finished
   (2) worth $1.00. So the finished
   (3) worth $1.00, or the finished
   (4) worth $1.00; therefore, the finished
   (5) worth $1.00, but the finished

8. Sentence 8: After the process is finished the can maker pays tax only on the $3.00 valued added to the product.

   What correction should be made to this sentence?

   (1) Replace *pays tax only* with *only pays tax*.
   (2) Change *after* to *since*.
   (3) Insert a comma after *process*.
   (4) Insert a comma after *finished*.
   (5) No correction is necessary.

9. Sentence 9: When the Beverage Company fills the $4.00 cans to make them worth $10.00, it pays tax on the $6.00 added value.

   What corrections should be made to this sentence?

   (1) Insert a comma after *cans*.
   (2) Change *it pays* to *they pay*.
   (3) Change *Beverage Company* to *beverage company*.
   (4) Replace *fills* with *fill*.
   (5) No correction is necessary.

10. Sentences 10 and 11: When you and I buy the canned beverage, we pay no <u>tax. Except</u>, of course, indirectly through increased prices.

    Which of the following is the best way to write the underlined portion of these sentences? If you think the original is the best way, choose option (1).

    (1) tax. Except,
    (2) tax, but except,
    (3) tax; except,
    (4) tax, except,
    (5) tax except,

Answers

The following gives both answers and explanations, including explanations about why wrong answers are wrong. You will also find references (by chapter and part) to specific rules, hints, and warnings. By checking the references, you can see how the GED test applies what you have studied so far.

1. Correct: **(3)** Use *between* to talk about two items and *among* to talk about more than two. See Chapter 13.

   Incorrect answers: (1) The singular subject *one* requires the singular verb *is*. See Chapter 3, Problem 1. (2) To add an apostrophe means to show ownership or the omission of a letter. Neither is the case here. See Chapter 11, Part 2. (4) A comma after *planners* would incorrectly separate the subject from the verb. See Chapter 9, Rule 5.

2. Correct: **(5)** The sentence is correct as it stands.

   Incorrect answers: (1) *Many* is always plural. *Tax*, however, is singular; so *much* is correct. See Chapter 3, Problem 2, Group B. (2) To add an apostrophe means to show ownership or the omission of a letter. Neither is the case here. See Chapter 11, Part 2. (3) A comma after *experts* would incorrectly separate the subject from the verb. See Chapter 2. (4) *To* must be followed by a noun or a verb. *Too* means "excessive." See Chapter 13.

3. Correct: **(1)** The pronoun *they* must agree with *experts*. So the verb must be *believe* to agree with *they*. See Chapter 4, Rule 10.

   Incorrect answers: (2) Use only the *-er* ending or the word *more*. See Chapter 5, Rule 7, Part A. (3) Do not separate the main clause from the noun clause. See both Chapter 8, Part 1, and Chapter 9, Summary. (4) *Are* is a plural verb and will not agree with the singular subject *tax*. See Chapter 3.

4. Correct: **(2)** *Tax* is singular, so all that follows must be singular: the verb *is*, the pronoun *one*, and the verb *taxes*. See Chapter 3, Problem 2, and Chapter 4, Rule 2.

   Incorrect answers: (1) *That taxes* is singular, but the word to which *that* refers is plural: *those*. So *that tax* is correct. See Chapter 4, Rule 10. (3) A comma here separates the subject from its verb, never a correct use of the comma. See Chapter 9, Summary. (4) *Are* is present tense (today). Keep present tense since other verbs in the passage are also present tense. See Chapter 1, Part 2.

5. Correct: **(1)** *It's* means "it is," not the intent here. See Chapter 13.

   Incorrect answers: (2) *For instance* is an introductory element and needs the comma. See Chapter 9, Rule 5. (3) *Pays* must agree with the subject *company*. See Chapter 3, Problem 1. (4) *Only* refers to *on the value*, so it is placed correctly. See Chapter 5 and, later, Chapter 16, Problem 3.

6. Correct: **(4)** The colon means "explanation follows." See Chapter 10, Part 2.

   Incorrect answers: (1) *It works* refers correctly to *value-added tax*. See Chapter 4. (2) *Here's* means "Here is." See Chapter 13. (3) The verb *is*, as in *here's*, agrees with the subject *it*. See Chapter 3, Problem 1.

7. Correct: **(5)** The comma and joining word correctly join the two parts of a compound sentence. See Chapter 9, Rule 3.

   Incorrect answers: (1) The omission of the comma at the end of the first sentence is incorrect. See Chapter 9, Rule 3. (2) The joining word *so* is illogical. In addition to Chapter 9, see also, later, Chapter 15, Part 2. (3) Again, the joining word *or* is illogical. (4) Although the use of the semicolon is technically correct, the joining word *therefore* is illogical.

8. Correct: **(4)** Use a comma after an introductory clause. See Chapter 9, Rule 5.

   Incorrect answers: (1) *Only* describes *on the $3.00* and so is correctly placed nearest that phrase. See Chapter 1, Part 4. (2) *Since* shows result; the correct relationship is *after*, referring to time. See Chapter 8, Part 3. (3) The entire introductory clause is *After the process is finished*, so no comma should break it. See Chapter 9, Rule 5.

9. Correct: **(3)** Capitalize only specific company names. See Chapter 12.

   Incorrect answers: (1) The entire introductory clause is *When the beverage company fills the $4.00 cans to make them worth $10.00,* so no comma should break it. See Chapter 9, Rule 5. (2) *It pays* is singular and correctly refers to the singular *company*. See Chapter 4, Rule 10. (4) *Fills*, a singular verb, agrees with the singular subject *company*. See Chapter 4, Rule 10.

10. Correct: **(5)** *Except* is a preposition, and what follows is a prepositional phrase. There is no rule to separate prepositional phrases from the rest of the sentence unless they are introductory. See Chapter 9, Summary.

    Incorrect answers: (1) *Except, of course, indirectly through increased prices* is a sentence fragment. It has no subject and verb. See Chapter 2 and, later, Chapter 16, Problem 6. (2) The joining word *but* is illogical. It does not join two compound parts. See Chapter 2, Compound Parts. (3) The semicolon is incorrect. It does not join two complete sentences. See Chapter 10, Part 1. (4) The comma is incorrect. See "Correct" above.

V

SENTENCES

V

SENTENCES

15

BASIC SENTENCE STRUCTURES

The whole point of studying different kinds of sentences is to learn to write them. Why? One mark of good writing is the use of a variety of sentence structures, and people who evaluate GED writing samples look for that variety.

Only four basic sentence structures make up the entire English language:

simple sentence
compound sentence
complex sentence
compound-complex sentence

This chapter teaches you to identify each and then to write each correctly.

PART 1: SIMPLE SENTENCES

The basic sentence is the simple sentence. It has the following characteristics:

1. The simple sentence has one subject.
2. It has one verb.
3. It may or may not have words or phrases telling about the subject or verb.

EXAMPLE: Randall overslept.
                subject: Randall
                verb: overslept
                words about the subject: (none)
                words about the verb: (none)

   Warning: Be sure the verb in your simple sentence can stand alone.

Error: Randall oversleeping.
            (The sentence is incomplete because the verb cannot stand alone.)
Revision: Randall has been oversleeping.
            (Now the simple sentence is accurate, with a single subject and a single verb.)

Hint: Since some verbs need helping words, a single verb may include more than one word.

EXAMPLE: Randall has been oversleeping.
subject: Randall
verb: has been oversleeping
(The main verb *oversleeping* and its helpers *has* and *been* make up a single verb, sometimes called a verb phrase. See Chapter 2 for a review.)

Although most sentences contain far more than a single subject and a single verb, many are still simple sentences.

EXAMPLE: Randall, my neighbor, overslept yesterday morning.
subject: Randall
verb: overslept
words about the subject: my neighbor (tells *who* about *Randall*)
words about the verb: yesterday morning (tells *when* about *overslept*)

EXAMPLE: Tomorrow evening, hoping to avoid oversleeping again, Randall will carefully set the alarm for 6:45 AM.
subject: Randall
verb: will set
words about the subject: (none)
words about the verb: tomorrow evening (tells *when* about *set*) hoping to avoid oversleeping again (tells *why* about *set*) carefully (tells *how* about *set*) the alarm (tells *what* about *set*) for 6:45 AM (tells *when* about *set*)

As you can see, then, even though a sentence may be relatively long, if it has only one subject and one verb, it is still a simple sentence.

 Remember: Length will not help identify the kind of sentence.

Sentence variety is a mark of the good writer, so as you write, you will want to vary your sentences. You have already seen that you can vary the length, but you can also vary the kinds of sentences you use. Now that you understand what a simple sentence is, let's talk about compound sentences.

PART 2: COMPOUND PARTS AND COMPOUND SENTENCES

Anything compound is made of two or more parts, so a compound sentence is made of two or more parts. The parts work as a single unit. Simple sentences can have compound subjects or compound verbs. Two simple sentences can be joined to form a compound sentence.

Compound Subjects

Sometimes a simple sentence has two subjects. The sentence is then said to have a compound subject.

EXAMPLE: Maria and Sue Ellen are going to the movie tonight.
two subjects: Maria, Sue Ellen
verb: are going

EXAMPLE: Five neighbors, a police officer, and two business owners formed a neighborhood committee to work for better streets.
three subjects: neighbors, officer, owners
verb: formed

⇨ **Warning: A plural subject is not a compound subject.**

EXAMPLE: Michael and David landed jobs at the same local supermarket.
two subjects: Michael and David
verb: landed
(The subject is compound because two nouns, *Michael* and *David*, are the subjects.)

EXAMPLE: Two brothers landed jobs at the same local supermarket.
one subject: brothers
verb: landed
(The subject is plural, not compound. Because only one noun, *brothers*, is the subject, the subject is not compound.)

Compound Verbs

Sometimes a simple sentence has two verbs. The sentence is then said to have a compound verb.

EXAMPLE: Smiles warm the heart and cheer the soul.
subject: smiles
two verbs: warm and cheer

EXAMPLE: The supervisor praises and rewards good, speedy work.
subject: supervisor
two verbs: praises and rewards

Compound Sentences

Sometimes a sentence is made by joining two simple sentences. The result is a compound sentence.

EXAMPLE: Randall overslept, so he was late for work.
sentence 1 subject: Randall
sentence 1 verb: overslept
sentence 2 subject: he
sentence 2 verb: was

NOTE: When you join two sentences, add a comma at the end of the first sentence. Notice the comma after *overslept* in the compound sentence above.

EXAMPLE: Maria and Sue Ellen are going to the movie tonight, but Lennie or Carol will stay home to baby-sit.
sentence 1: Maria and Sue Ellen are going to the movie tonight.
sentence 2: Lennie or Carol will stay home to baby-sit.

As you can see from the above examples, when two simple sentences are joined together, they form a compound sentence.

 Remember: Use a comma to replace the period at the end of the first sentence, in front of the joining word, when you hook together two sentences. (See Commas, Rule 3, for a review.)

Common joining words are as follows:

and   but   or   nor   for   yet   so

 Warning 1: Be sure to use the joining words correctly. Study the following meanings and examples.

And means "also" and joins two equal ideas: this idea *and* that idea.

EXAMPLE: Repairing the dented fender will be expensive, and I have no insurance.

 Remember: The comma replaces the period at the end of the first sentence, in front of *and*.

But shows a difference, an exception, a change: this idea *but* not that idea.

EXAMPLE: The storm damaged the roof, but the rest of the house was unhurt.

Or shows an alternative: this idea *or* that idea.

EXAMPLE: You should cover the windshield, or you will have to scrape off ice and snow in the morning.

Nor means "neither." Like *or*, *nor* shows an alternative, but both alternatives are negative: neither this idea *nor* that idea.

EXAMPLE: The doctor's report sounded bad, nor did the nurse have anything good to say.

For means "because" or "for this reason."

EXAMPLE: The turtle soup was nutritious, for it was thick with meat and vegetables.

So means "with the result that": this is true, *so* that is true.

EXAMPLE: Road construction narrowed the usual two lanes to one, so traffic slowed to a snail's pace.

⇨   **Warning 2: Be sure to distinguish between joining words that merely connect two subjects or two verbs and those that connect two sentences. Use commas only with those that connect two sentences.**

EXAMPLE: Company officials hope to cash in on the rising market trends *and* make significant profit gains as a result.
one subject: officials
two verbs: hope and make
(*And* joins two verbs, not two sentences. Use no comma.)

EXAMPLE: Company officials hope to cash in on the rising market trends, *and* they may make significant profit gains as a result.
sentence 1:   Company officials hope to cash in on the rising market trends.
sentence 2:   They may make significant profit gains as a result.
joining word: and
(The comma appears at the end of the first sentence, in front of *and*.)

⇨   **Warning 3: If you omit the joining word when you hook two sentences together, you commit a serious error. We call that error a *comma splice* or *comma fault*. In other words, you must not join two sentences with only a comma. Use *both* the comma and a joining word.**

Error: Rigorous walking strengthens the cardiovascular system, jogging does the same thing.
(two sentences incorrectly joined with a comma)

Revision: Rigorous walking strengthens the cardiovascular system, and jogging does the same thing.
(two sentences joined with *and* and a comma forming a compound sentence)

✎   **Remember: You may use a semicolon to join two sentences if the joining word is omitted. (Review use of semicolons in Chapter 10, Part 1.)**

EXAMPLE: Rigorous walking strengthens the cardiovascular system; jogging does the same thing.
(two sentences joined with a semicolon to form a compound sentence)

PART 3: COMPLEX SENTENCES

The word *complex* generally means "complicated." Complex sentences, as you might guess, are indeed complicated. Complex sentences have the following characteristics:

1. A complex sentence contains at least two clauses.
2. One clause must be the independent clause.
3. One or more clauses must be dependent clauses.

Independent Clauses

A clause is a group of words with a subject and a verb. (Review Chapter 8.)

☞ **Hint 1: A simple sentence is a clause.**

EXAMPLE: The race began.
  subject: race
  verb: began

When the subject and verb make a sentence, this clause is an *independent clause*. We call it "independent" because, like an independent person, it can support itself. It can stand alone. Sometimes we call the independent clause the "main" clause. It's like the "main" man or woman in a household.

Dependent Clauses

Sometimes a group of words with a subject and verb does not make a sentence. That is, it cannot stand alone.

EXAMPLE: When the whistle sounded
  subject: whistle
  verb: sounded

EXAMPLE: Because the traffic had slowed to a stop
  subject: traffic
  verb: had slowed

A clause that cannot stand alone is called a *dependent clause*. We call it "dependent" because, like a dependent person, it needs support to survive. A dependent clause needs—depends on—an independent clause for its meaning. Remember this two-part comparison:

1. An independent clause (main clause) is like the head of the household—the "main" person.
2. A dependent clause is like a child—a dependent.

EXAMPLE: Because the traffic had slowed to a stop, I knew I would be late for work.
  dependent clause: because the traffic had slowed to a stop
  independent clause: I knew I would be late for work.

Now the dependent clause has meaning. It explains *why* about the independent clause.

Joined Clauses

When an independent clause and a dependent clause are joined in a sentence, the sentence is complex.

EXAMPLE: When the whistle sounded, the race began.
  independent clause: The race began.
  dependent clause: When the whistle sounded

Warning: If you write a dependent clause as if it were a sentence, you commit a serious writing error. We call that error a sentence fragment. Be sure every sentence includes an independent (main) clause.

Three kinds of dependent clauses appear in complex sentences:

noun clauses
adjective clauses
adverb clauses

You may need to review the three kinds of clauses in detail in Chapter 8, but here are some examples:

Noun Clause

The noun clause functions any way a noun functions. It can be a subject, an object, or a predicate word.

EXAMPLE: The salesman talked to *whoever* would listen.
independent clause: The salesman talked
dependent clause: whoever would listen
(The dependent clause *whoever would listen* is a noun clause that is the object of the word *to* in the independent clause.)

Adjective Clause

An adjective clause functions the way adjectives function; it tells *which one, what kind,* or *how many* about a noun.

EXAMPLE: We joined Teresa, who was sitting alone.
independent clause: We joined Teresa.
dependent clause: who was sitting alone
(The dependent clause *who was sitting alone* is an adjective clause that tells *which one* about the noun *Teresa.*)

Adverb Clause

Adverb clauses modify verbs, adjectives, and other adverbs. They answer questions like *when? where? how? why?* and *to what extent?*

EXAMPLE: After we ate dinner, we played softball.
(The clause *after we ate dinner* tells *when* about the verb *played.* Any word that tells *when* about a verb is an adverb.)

 Warning: Sometimes what seems to be an introductory word is *not* followed by both a subject and a verb. In that case you do not have an adverb clause.

EXAMPLE: After eating dinner, we played softball.
independent clause: We played softball.
dependent clause: (none)
(The sentence has no dependent clause. No subject or verb follows the word *after,* a word that often is an introductory word. *After eating dinner* is only a prepositional phrase.)

 Remember: A clause must have both a subject and a verb.

PART 4: COMPOUND-COMPLEX SENTENCES

The compound-complex sentence will be easy for you because it is the combination of two kinds of sentences you already know.

$$\frac{\text{simple}}{\text{sentence}} + \frac{\text{complex}}{\text{sentence}} = \frac{\text{compound-complex}}{\text{sentence}}$$

EXAMPLE:

simple sentence: My car made a funny noise.
complex sentence: The mechanic used a computer to find out what was wrong.
    independent clause: The mechanic used a computer to find out.
    dependent clause: what was wrong
compound-complex: My car made a funny noise, so the mechanic used a computer to find out what was wrong.

Or to put it another way,

$$\frac{\text{independent}}{\text{clause}} + \frac{\text{independent}}{\text{clause}} + \frac{\text{dependent}}{\text{clause}} = \frac{\text{compound-complex}}{\text{sentence}}$$

The compound-complex sentence *must* include a dependent clause in one of its independent clauses, but it *may* include a dependent clause in *both* independent clauses:

EXAMPLE:

complex sentence: Since minimum wages increased, I need work only one job.
    independent clause: I need work only one job.
    dependent clause: Since minimum wages increased
complex sentence: Now I have time to take extra classes that will help me improve my skills.
    independent clause: Now I have time to take extra classes.
    dependent clause: That will help me improve my skills
compound-complex: Since minimum wages increased, I need work only one job; so now I have time to take extra classes that will help me improve my skills.

RULE: In a compound sentence, use a semicolon at the end of the first sentence if other commas appear in the first sentence. (See also Chapter 10, Part 1, Rule B.)

EXAMPLE: When you use a computer only for games, you miss the real capability of the technology; but after you put in a day's work at the keyboard, you may no longer thrill to the games.
    first dependent clause: you/use
    first independent clause: you/miss
    second dependent clause: you/put
    second independent clause: you/may thrill

To see if you understand what this chapter is about, try your hand with the following exercises.

PRACTICE

Exercise 1

Directions: Identify the following sentences as simple (S), compound (CD), complex (CX), or compound-complex (CC). Some simple sentences will have compound subjects or compound verbs, so be sure to identify those as such. Answers follow below, but don't peek until you've completed your answers. Then you can decide if you understand!

1. Walking is good exercise.

2. When conditions are right, I really enjoy fishing for bass.

3. The plant foreman and the union steward investigated the workman's complaint.

4. Job applications call for accuracy and neatness.

5. Seeking a new job, Leroy answered newspaper ads and applied in person.

6. The clothing department featured the newest styles, but Janice hoped to find something more conservative.

7. If you understand its operation, a wood lathe can be a useful tool; but if you are untrained, you can be seriously hurt by it.

8. As we studied the almost perfect reflections in the lake, we felt dizzy.

9. After studying the almost perfect reflections in the lake, we felt dizzy.

10. Hamburgers and fries are popular fast foods.

11. The vocal trio needed more practice, so the recital was postponed.

12. Sherry and Marcella bus tables at a local restaurant, but unless they can work shorter hours, they will feel obligated to find different jobs.

13. The secretary took Mr. Toon's calls while he was in the three-hour meeting.

14. The secretary took Mr. Toon's calls during the three-hour meeting.

15. After the three-hour meeting, Mr. Toon returned his calls.

Exercise 1—Answers

1. simple (walking/is)

2. complex (introductory word, *when*; dependent clause, conditions/are; independent clause, I/enjoy)

3. simple with compound subject (foreman and steward/investigated)

4. simple (applications/call)

5. simple with compound verb (Leroy/answered and applied)

6. compound (department/featured; Janice/hoped; joining word, *but* with comma at end of first clause)

7. compound-complex (introductory word, *if*; dependent clause, you/understand; independent clause, lathe/can be; joining word, *but*; second introductory word, *if*; second dependent clause, you/are; second independent clause, you/can be)

8. complex (introductory word, *as*; dependent clause, we/studied; independent clause, we/felt)

9. simple (we/felt; *after* is not an introductory word since no subject follows)

10. simple with compound subject (hamburgers, fries/are)

11. compound (trio/needed; recital/was postponed; joining word, *so* with comma at end of first clause)

12. compound-complex (independent clause, Sherry, Marcella/bus; joining word, *but*; introductory word, *unless*; dependent clause, they/can work; independent clause, they/will feel)

13. complex (independent clause, secretary/took; introductory word, *while*; dependent clause, he/was)

14. simple (secretary/took)

15. simple (Mr. Toon/returned; *after* is not an introductory word because no verb follows)

Exercise 2

Directions: Put the following sentences together to make new ones. Be sure to use necessary punctuation.

> *Example: Join these sentences to make a complex sentence:*
> a. *Cotton fields stretched as far as the eye could see.*
> b. *I was surprised.*
> *Answer: I was surprised that cotton fields stretched as far as the eye could see.*

1. Put these sentences together to make a compound sentence:
   a. We stopped to talk to the park ranger.
   b. He warned us about the rattlesnakes along the trails.

2. Join the same two sentences into a complex sentence.

3. Join these sentences to make a complex sentence:
   a. The logging trucks were loaded and chained.
   b. Then the logging trucks rumbled down the highway.

4. Join the same two sentences into a simple sentence.

5. Combine these sentences into a complex sentence. Write two dependent clauses and one independent clause.
   a. Over-the-road drivers travel long distances.
   b. Over-the-road drivers sometimes do not take breaks.
   c. They sometimes fall asleep at the wheel.

6. Use the same three sentences above to write a simple sentence with a compound verb.

7. Combine these sentences to make a complex sentence:
   a. Maria rode the subway about thirty blocks.
   b. Then Maria walked another eight blocks.
   c. Maria reached the place for the job interview.

8. Use the same three sentences above to write a compound-complex sentence.

9. Join these sentences into one simple sentence. The sentence will have compound parts.
   a. Julio had carpenter's tools.
   b. He had plumber's tools.

    c. He had electrician's tools.

    d. He had all the tools stored in his truck.

    e. He knew how to use them all.

10. Use the same set of sentences above to create a compound sentence.

Exercise 2—Answers

1. We stopped to talk to the park ranger, and he warned us about the rattlesnakes along the trails. (Be sure you used a comma to replace the period at the end of the first clause.)

2. We stopped to talk to the park ranger who warned us about the rattlesnakes along the trails.

3. After the logging trucks were loaded and chained, they rumbled down the highway. (Did you use a comma after the introductory element? See Rule 5 in Chapter 9.)

4. The logging trucks, loaded and chained, rumbled down the highway.

5. When over-the-road drivers travel long distances or when they do not take breaks, they sometimes fall asleep at the wheel. (Did you use a comma correctly?)

6. Over-the-road drivers travel long distances, sometimes do not take breaks, and sometimes fall asleep at the wheel.

7. After Maria rode the subway for about thirty blocks and walked another eight, she reached the place for the job interview. (Check punctuation.)

8. Maria rode the subway for about thirty blocks; and after she walked another eight blocks, she reached the place for the job interview. (Did you use either a comma or a semicolon where you joined the two main clauses?)

9. Julio had carpenter's tools, plumber's tools, and electrician's tools stored in his truck and knew how to use them all. (Did you use commas to separate the items in the series? See Rule 1 in Chapter 9.)

10. Julio had carpenter's tools, plumber's tools, and electrician's tools stored in his truck; he knew how to use them all. (Be sure to use both the commas for the series and a semicolon between the compound sentences.)

Exercise 3

Directions: Most of the following sentences are incorrect. Some are joined incorrectly; some are incomplete sentences (dependent clauses without independent clauses); some are correct. Correct any errors.

1. Cartoon character Bugs Bunny is now fifty years old and so is Mickey Mouse.

2. A computer keyboard looks very much like a typewriter keyboard, people who use one can use the other.

3. Air pollution and water pollution are big political issues candidates like to make voters believe they are all friends of the environment.

4. After the security officer made hourly checks.

5. Because they make money, movie sequels are popular among producers and actors.

6. While we were visiting the pet cemetery.

7. After we visited the pet cemetery near the edge of town but near our house.

8. As the gas station attendant made change, we recalled the days when "self-serve" was the exception, not the rule.

9. Microwave ovens are real time savers, they cook food in minutes.

10. Windmills used to supply most of the electricity on many western ranches, now more modern windmills still produce energy-efficient power.

Exercise 3—Answers

1. old, (two sentences put together with only a joining word; add comma. See Rule 3, Chapter 9.)

2. keyboard, so *or* keyboard; people (two sentences joined with only a comma; add joining word or use semicolon. See Chapter 10, Part 1.)

3. issues; *or* issues, so (two sentences joined with nothing; use semicolon or use comma and joining word. See Chapter 10, Part 1.)

4. Answers will vary. Suggestion: After the security officer made hourly checks, he filed a report. (no independent clause; add one.)

5. (correct)

6. Answers will vary. Suggestion: I felt sad while we were visiting the pet cemetery. (no independent clause; add one.)

7. Answers will vary. Suggestion: After we visited the pet cemetery near the edge of town but still near our house, we decided to bury our own pet there. (no independent clause; add one.)

8. (correct)

9. savers; *or* savers, for (two sentences joined without joining word; use either semicolon or comma *and* joining word. See Rule 3 in Chapter 9 and Part 1 in Chapter 10.)

10. ranches; *or* ranches, and (two sentences joined without joining word; use either semicolon or comma and joining word.

Exercise 4

Directions: Now that you can identify kinds of sentences, try your hand at writing them. Below are directions for writing a variety of sentence structures. See what you can do with the skeletons provided. It is fair to warn you that the items become progressively more difficult, but with some practice, you'll be ready for the tough ones when you get to them! (That's a compound-complex sentence you just read!)

1. Write a simple sentence with *employees* as the subject and *work* as the verb.

2. Write a simple sentence with two subjects and one verb. Use *taking tests* as one subject.

3. Write a simple sentence with one subject and two verbs. Use *sunshine* as the subject.

4. Write a simple sentence with two subjects and two verbs. Use *Uncle Clyde* and *Aunt Thelma* as the two subjects.

5. Write a compound sentence with *watermelon* as one subject and *tastes* as one verb. Be sure to use a comma at the end of the first clause.

6. Write another compound sentence with *car* as one subject and *runs* as one verb. Use a different joining word than you did for sentence 5. Be sure to use a comma to separate the two sentences.

7. Write a complex sentence using *Cecil walked* as the subject and verb of the independent clause. Begin the dependent adverb clause with *because*.

8. Write a complex sentence using *Cecil walked* as the subject and verb of the dependent clause. Make the dependent clause an adverb clause and put it at the beginning of the sentence.

9. Rewrite sentence 8 and put the dependent adverb clause at the end of the sentence.

10. Write a complex sentence using an adjective clause to describe the subject *sister*.

Exercise 4—Answers

The following answers are only patterns after which your own sentences should be formed. The italicized parts are required. Otherwise, you should have the same series of independent and dependent clauses. Above all, if you have similar patterns, you have proved that you can write some really sophisticated sentences. Good for you!

1. Good *employees* usually *work* beyond the minimum task.

2. Interviewing for jobs and *taking tests* make some people nervous.

3. *Sunshine* makes me happy and keeps me warm.

4. On Sundays, *Uncle Clyde* and *Aunt Thelma* usually eat dinner at a local restaurant famous for barbecue.

5. During hot summer afternoons, ice-cold *watermelon tastes* better than anything else, but during cold winter evenings, hot chocolate hits the spot.

6. The antique *car runs* only thirty-five miles per hour, so it can't enter most interstate highways.

7. *Because* he had a flat tire and no spare, *Cecil walked* the last three miles home.

8. Because *Cecil walked* three miles in the rain, he was soaked to the skin.

9. Cecil was soaked to the skin because he walked three miles in the rain.

10. Carolyn's *sister*, who won first place in the dance contest, hopes to compete in more dance contests.

16

COMMON SENTENCE PROBLEMS

Sentences are the building blocks of any piece of writing, whether for your job, your personal life, or the GED essay. If you can write one good sentence, you can write two. If you can write two, you can write three. And if you can write three, finally you have a complete piece of writing—all of it good! This chapter will help you solve common sentence problems.

PROBLEM 1: USING SPECIFIC WORDS

Without specific words, an otherwise good sentence fails.

Identifying Vague Words

When writing "lacks specifics," usually the writer has used only vague words to try to get across his message. You have a picture in your mind of what you are trying to say. Try turning the tables, and imagine the message your reader is getting. Are you putting the picture in your mind into your reader's mind?

EXAMPLE: We toured a big building.

Your reader has no picture of "building." Is this an office building, a church, a school, or something else? What do you mean by "big"? Is it six stories tall, seventy-five stories tall, or just one story tall but spread across fifty acres?

EXAMPLE: Today is a miserable day.

Your reader needs specifics. Is the day miserable because of the weather—rain, ice storm, hot, humid, cloudy? Or is the day miserable because you have a bad cold or everything seems to be going wrong?

☞   Hint: *Show* your reader; don't *tell* him. *Show* him a big building, a miserable day. Don't simply *tell* him the building is big or the day miserable.

Replacing Vague Words

Let's use the same examples above and create good pictures for the reader's mind.

EXAMPLE: We toured a big building.

Revisions: We toured a 75-story office building that had three floors underground.
We toured a church that covers a city block and whose spire rises above all other buildings in the city.
We toured a high school that sprawls across eighty acres.

EXAMPLE: Today is a miserable day.

Revisions: With the temperature edging near 100 degrees, my shirt is clinging to me, the sweat running down my scalp, pasting my hair to my head and neck and burning my eyes.
Today I lost my job, had a fender-bender accident on my way home, and then spilled a cup of hot chocolate on the white carpet.

Make sure when you write that you put the picture in your reader's mind.

   Remember: Don't tell your reader; show him.

PROBLEM 2: COMBINING SENTENCES

The GED tests your ability to put sentences together correctly in two ways. One way is in questions like the following:

Sentences 1 and 2: The cost of new homes is high today. Many people are purchasing older homes in need of renovation.

The most effective combination of sentences 1 and 2 would include which of the following groups of words?

   (1) Although many homes need renovation

(2) Although the cost of new homes is high today

(3) Because many people are purchasing older homes

(4) Because the cost of new homes is high today

(5) purchase older homes in need of renovation

(Answer: 4)

The second way, of course, is in your essay response. So let's study some correct ways to combine sentences.

Method 1:   Join adjectives.

Sometimes you can create new, improved sentences by joining adjectives.

EXAMPLE: The paper is wet.
The paper is torn.
The paper is useless for wrapping anything.

Combined: The *wet, torn* paper is useless for wrapping anything.
(See Chapter 9, Rule 2, for comma rules.)

Method 2:   Use appositives.

An appositive is a noun that renames another noun. You can join two sentences by making one an appositive.

EXAMPLE: My uncle is a ten-year veteran in the fire department.
My uncle has made me conscious of fire hazards in the home.

Combined: My uncle, *a ten-year veteran in the fire department*, has made me conscious of fire hazards in the home.

⇨ Warning: Appositives are set off from the rest of the sentence with commas. (See Chapter 9, Rule 6A.)

Method 3:   Use phrases.

Often two sentences can be combined by making one of them into a participial phrase. (See Chapter 7, Part 3.)

⇨ Warning: Often, the participle is set off with commas, but participles that are necessary to identify the words they modify have no commas. (See Chapter 9, Rule 4.)

EXAMPLE: The package is lying on the counter.
The package belongs to me.

Combined: The package *lying on the counter* belongs to me.
(No commas are necessary since *lying on the counter* identifies which package.)

EXAMPLE: My car is parked illegally.
My car may be towed away.

Combined: My car, *parked illegally*, may be towed away.
(The commas indicate added information. The writer has only one car, so *parked illegally* is not needed to identify which car.)

☞ Hint: Participles can appear at the beginning, in the middle, or at the end of a sentence. Hence, they give many ways to achieve sentence variety.

Method 4:   Use clauses.

Clauses are groups of words that have both a subject and a verb. (See Chapters 8 and 15.) Using dependent clauses will help you combine sentences.

EXAMPLE: Some bicycles have training wheels.
Some bicycles help beginners learn to ride.

Combined: Bicycles *that have training wheels* help beginners learn to ride.

Since some clauses are movable, consider the alternatives for combining these sentences:

EXAMPLE: The snow was deep.
The depth was fourteen inches.
We could not move the car.
We had to shovel out the driveway.

Combined: *Because the snow was fourteen inches deep, we could not move the car until we shoveled out the driveway.*

Varied: *Until we shoveled out the driveway, we could not move the car because the snow was fourteen inches deep.*

Varied: *We could not move the car until we shoveled out the driveway because the snow was fourteen inches deep.*

Varied: *Because the snow was fourteen inches deep, until we shoveled out the driveway, we could not move the car.*

PROBLEM 3: PLACING WORDS CORRECTLY

Sometimes a word or phrase is placed next to a word that it cannot describe in a way that makes sense. Correct the problem by changing or moving the word or phrase. (See also Chapter 7, Part 3C.)

Incorrect: Running around the block, the building came into view.
(The building is not running around the block.)
Correct: Running around the block, I saw the building come into view.

Incorrect: Rodney told Angela not to get upset calmly.
Correct: Rodney calmly told Angela not to get upset.
(*Calmly* talks about *told* and so should be placed as near to *told* as possible.)

PROBLEM 4: BALANCING SETS OF WORDS

When you put groups of words together, they need balance. To give them balance, write them with similar words.

Unbalanced: Carol likes *basketball* and *attending football games*.
Balanced: Carol likes *basketball* and *football*.

Unbalanced: Mark *studied* grammar and *his answers were checked*.
Balanced: Mark *studied* grammar and *checked* his answers.

Unbalanced: Sandra was *tall* and *with blond hair*.
Balanced: Sandra was *tall* and *blond*.

Unbalanced: *Working regular hours* and *to be able to pay the rent* were my goals.
Balanced: *Working regular hours* and *being able to pay the rent* were my goals.

PROBLEM 5: AVOIDING RUN-ONS AND COMMA SPLICES

A run-on sentence occurs when two sentences are joined without a connecting word or any punctuation.

Run-on Sentence: The man ambled aimlessly through the crowd the woman walked with a purpose.

Corrected: The man ambled aimlessly through the crowd, but the woman walked with a purpose.

Corrected: The man ambled aimlessly through the crowd; the woman walked with a purpose.

☞ Hint: To correct a run-on sentence, use one of two methods:
(1) Join the sentences with a comma and a joining word.
(Review Chapter 15, Part 2.)
(2) Join the sentences with a semicolon.
(See Chapter 10, Part 1)

A comma splice occurs when two sentences are joined (spliced together) with only a comma.

Comma splice: The man ambled aimlessly through the crowd, the woman walked with a purpose.

Corrected: The man ambled aimlessly through the crowd, but the woman walked with a purpose.

☞ Hint: To join two sentences correctly, use either a comma *and* a joining word or use a semicolon.

PROBLEM 6: AVOIDING SENTENCE FRAGMENTS

A sentence fragment is part of a sentence. If you punctuate part of a sentence as if it were a complete sentence, you make a serious error. There are two common kinds of fragments.

TYPE 1: Phrase as fragment

Fragment: We saw the car. Speeding down the expressway.
Corrected: We saw the car speeding down the expressway.

☞ Hint 1: To correct the fragment, join the phrase to the main clause it describes.

Fragment: After working all day in the sun. He needed to drink plenty of liquids.
Corrected: After working all day in the sun, he needed to drink plenty of liquids.

☞   Hint 2: To correct some fragments, change the verbal to a verb.
(See Chapter 7.)

Fragment: The waves lapping against the shore in a quiet, sleepy rhythm.
Corrected: The waves lapped against the shore in a quiet, sleepy rhythm.

TYPE 2:   Dependent clause as fragment

Fragment: I found my shop coat on the floor. When I arrived for work.
Corrected: I found my shop coat on the floor when I arrived for work.

☞   Hint 3: To correct dependent clause fragments, join them to a main clause.

☞   Hint 4: The best way to find fragments is to read your paper *backwards* sentence by sentence. In most cases, you will then be able to recognize pieces of sentences that cannot stand alone.

PRACTICE

Exercise 1

Directions: Revise the following sentences to eliminate vague words. You will find more than one vague word in each sentence. As you revise, don't tell your reader; show him!

1. A tall man came into the room. (Clarify the vague words *tall*, *man*, *came*, and *room*.)

2. The child played with her toys. (Clarify *child*, *played*, and *toys*.)

3. The car wasn't running well. (Clarify *car* and *wasn't running well*.)

4. That man is really dirty! (Clarify *that man* and *dirty*.)

5. I was too busy to finish my chores. (Clarify *too busy* and *chores*.)

6. I ate too much. (You're on your own now. You decide what needs to be clarified.)

7. Mariann was dressed funny.

8. Wilma's present came in a big box.

9. The paint matched the gaudy wallpaper.

10. We had fun at the picnic.

Exercise 1—Answers

The following are only suggested revisions for the ten sentences above. Obviously, yours will differ. If you've clarified the vague words in a similar manner, however, you know you're on the right track.

1. A seven-foot-tall basketball player ducked into the kitchen.

2. The toddler threw blocks across the room.

3. The 1967 jalopy clattered down the street in a cloud of blue smoke.

4. White spots where his goggles protected his eyes were the only places the miner was not covered with coal dust.

5. Because I worked until 11:30 last night, I didn't have time to do the laundry, wash the dishes, or iron a clean shirt.

6. I ate four hamburgers, three bowls of chili, a large pizza, and two combination salads.

7. Mariann wore men's hip boots, a fur coat, and a white ruffled sunbonnet.

8. Wilma's surprise birthday present came in a box the size of a 24-inch television set.

9. The purple paint matched the purple, pink, gray, and yellow wallpaper.

10. At the family reunion picnic, we played Frisbee, volleyball, and softball and ate off and on all afternoon.

Exercise 2

Directions: Vary the following sentences in at least three ways. You may use any sentence-combining technique you've learned.

1. Some men work in oil fields.
   These men are sometimes called "roughnecks."
   The name is appropriate for the job.

2. The highway crew arrived to clear the road.
   The road was strewn with boxes of nails.
   The nails spilled when a truck overturned.

3. Some people adore cats.
   Some people adore dogs.
   Few people adore both.
   Bitter arguments arise between the two.

4. Students are hard workers.
   Students are studious.
   Pupils merely attend classes.

5. Ona is on a diet.
   She ate chocolate chip cookies and ice cream.

Exercise 2—Answers

The following are suggested variations possible from the above.

1. a) Men who work in oil fields are sometimes called "roughnecks," an appropriate name for the job.
   b) Men who work in oil fields are sometimes called, appropriately, "roughnecks."
   c) "Roughnecks" is an appropriate name for the men who work in oil fields.

2. a) The highway crew arrived to clear the road which was strewn with boxes of nails when a truck overturned.
   b) After a truck overturned and spilled nails over the road, the highway crew arrived to clear the mess.
   c) The highway crew arrived to clear the road after a truck overturned and spilled boxes of nails on the highway.

3. a) Although some people adore cats and some adore dogs, few adore both, and bitter arguments arise between the two.
   b) Although few people adore both, some adore cats and others adore dogs, and bitter arguments arise between the two.
   c) Bitter arguments arise between the people who adore cats and others who adore dogs because few adore both.

4. a) While pupils merely attend classes, students are hard working and studious.
   b) Students are hardworking and studious while pupils merely attend classes.
   c) Pupils merely attend classes, but students are hard working and studious.

5. a) Even though Ona is on a diet, she ate chocolate chip cookies and ice cream.
   b) Even though she ate chocolate chip cookies and ice cream, Ona is on a diet.
   c) She ate chocolate chip cookies and ice cream, but Ona is on a diet.

Exercise 3

Directions: Rewrite these sentences to correct misplaced word(s).

1. Throwing the ball hard, the batter was struck by the pitcher.

2. To create the right color, the paint was mixed carefully.

3. Complaining of a headache, the doctor gave Jethrow medicine.

4. My boss ordered me back to work angrily.

5. After learning the basic rules, the game went smoothly.

6. We heard the board elected officers on the late news last night.

7. The cat played with the ball running in circles.

8. The students on the other side of the field, who are cheering wildly, are the team's loyal followers.

Exercise 3—Answers

1. Throwing the ball hard, the pitcher struck the batter.

2. To create the right color, he mixed the paint carefully.

3. Complaining of a headache, Jethrow received medicine from the doctor.

4. My boss angrily ordered me back to work.

5. After learning the basic rules, I smoothly played the game.

6. On the late news last night, we heard the board elected officers.

7. Running in circles, the cat played with the ball.

8. The students who are cheering wildly on the other side of the field are the team's loyal followers.

Exercise 4

Directions: Rewrite these sentences so the pairs or groups of words are balanced.

1. Shelton likes to play basketball, going to movies, and skiing.

2. They traveled by plane, in boats, and by train.

3. Cathy promised that she would cut the grass and to trim the hedges.

4. The best way to study is to find a quiet room and concentrating on the lesson.

5. Her goal was to become an accountant and attending classes in ethnic cooking.

6. Jennifer carried the boxes carefully and with ease.

7. To be cheerful and showing optimism are good qualities.

8. Erin planned a shopping trip and to go on a short vacation.

Exercise 4—Answers

1. Shelton likes basketball, movies, and skiing.

2. They traveled by plane, by boat, and by train.

3. Cathy promised that she would cut the grass and trim the hedges.

4. The best way to study is to find a quiet room and concentrate on the lesson.

5. Her goal was to become an accountant and attend classes in ethnic cooking.

6. Jennifer carried the boxes carefully and easily.

7. To be cheerful and to show optimism are good qualities.

8. Erin planned a shopping trip and a short vacation.

Exercise 5

Directions: Correct these sentences as needed. Some may be correct.

1. As we write, we must avoid comma splices, they are serious errors.

2. Run-on sentences are just as bad they are serious errors, too.

3. Writing effective sentences takes care but makes sense.

4. The neighbor's dogs howled all night, they kept me awake until 3:00 AM.

5. What he wants for his car is a new paint job, but what he will get for his car is just a good wax job.

6. In 1965 when gas was twenty-nine cents a gallon, we often took short family trips, now we take only one trip a year.

7. The table is too big for the room there is no room for any extra chairs.

8. The job of raking leaves kept Robert busy all day Saturday so he was happy to relax on Sunday.

9. The car windshields in the parking lot reflected the sunlight, and the reflection hurt my eyes.

10. The clothes dryer dries some of my shirts wrinkle-free, I iron most of them.

Exercise 5—Answers

1. comma splices; they OR comma splices; for

2. bad; they OR bad, for

3. correct

4. night, and OR night; they

5. correct

6. trips, but OR trips; now

7. room; there OR room, and

8. Saturday, so

9. correct

10. wrinkle-free, but

Exercise 6

Directions: Rewrite the following sentences to correct any sentence fragments. Some sentences may be correct.

1. Tina knew she would find the answer to the problem. When she left work today.

2. This new printer is really fast. It can print a full page in less than thirty seconds.

3. Whatever you need to get the job done.

4. Having spoken, he sat down.

5. Harold called yesterday. Thinking it was my birthday.

6. Across the patio, through the yard, and out the driveway.

7. The cars parked in the lot across the street from our house.

8. A soft, gentle breeze sighing through the pines and across our picnic table.

Exercise 6—Answers

1. Tina knew she would find the answer to the problem when she left work today.

2. correct

3. We will order whatever you need to get the job done.

4. correct

5. Harold called yesterday thinking it was my birthday.

6. I chased the new puppy across the patio, through the yard, and out the driveway.

7. The cars are parked in the lot across the street from our house.

8. A soft, gentle breeze sighed through the pines and across our picnic table.

CHECKLIST FOR WRITING EFFECTIVE SENTENCES

Use the following checklist to evaluate your own sentences. You should be able to answer yes to each of these questions.

	YES	NO
1. Have I started each sentence with a capital letter?	☐	☐
2. Have I used an end mark of punctuation—a period, a question mark, or an exclamation point?	☐	☐
3. Have I written complete sentences?	☐	☐
4. Have I avoided comma splices and run-on sentences?	☐	☐
5. Have I used a variety of simple, compound, complex, and compound-complex sentences?	☐	☐
6. Have I used specific, concrete words?	☐	☐
7. Have I placed words and phrases correctly so that they are next to the words they describe?	☐	☐
8. Have I balanced sets of words?	☐	☐
9. Have I punctuated correctly?	☐	☐

VI

PARAGRAPHS

17
STATEMENT OF PURPOSE

The writing you will do for the GED test is called an *essay*. An essay is a short piece of writing that tells what you think about something and gives details to explain your thoughts. You should begin your essay with a *statement of purpose*. That sentence does just what its name says: it states your purpose in writing the essay. Study the following examples:

Statement of Purpose: Getting along with fellow workers is important but sometimes difficult. (The writer will explain *how* to get along.)

Statement of Purpose: Regular exercise helps people feel better, think better, and work better. (The writer will explain *why* this is true.)

Statement of Purpose: Farm subsidies needlessly increase the cost of our groceries. (The writer will support this *opinion* by giving details to show why he thinks so.)

Statement of Purpose: There are both advantages and disadvantages to working at night. (The writer will give details to show both good and bad results from night jobs.)

Why start with a statement of purpose? Two reasons:

1. By starting with a statement of purpose, you force yourself to say exactly what you are going to do in your essay.
2. By starting with a statement of purpose, you tell your reader exactly what you are going to do in your essay.

What makes a good statement of purpose? In order to answer the question, let's compare some poor statements of purpose with better ones:

Poor: Last month I began taking a computer training class. (We can only guess what the writer will talk about: the class? the instructor? the equipment? the homework? the exhaustion from taking classes after working all day?)

Better: Computer training classes provide job training for an expanding job market. (We know the writer will explain why the classes are beneficial in terms of job potential.)

Poor: At my age, I still have the energy to work hard and play hard. (We assume the writer is going to talk about working and playing.)

Better: At my age, I have the energy to work and play hard, but I lack the experience for better jobs. (We know now that the writer will compare the advantages and disadvantages of youth in the job market.)

So, what makes a good statement of purpose? It should say in one sentence *exactly* what you are going to write about—exactly what you are going to explain—in your completed essay.

☞ Hint: The statement of purpose should *not* say, "The purpose of this essay is to. . . ." Rather, simply say what you are going to talk about.

EXAMPLE:

Poor: The purpose of this essay is to explain why I think drunk drivers should be imprisoned.

Better: Drunk drivers should be imprisoned.

Better: Drunk drivers should be imprisoned for three important reasons.

Before you write your own statements of purpose, work though the following exercise to see if you recognize the difference between good ones and poor ones.

PRACTICE

Exercise 1

Directions: Decide whether the following are good or poor statements of purpose. Compare your answers with those that follow.

1. Autumn is my favorite time of year.

2. Three area houses are built of Bedford stone.

3. Last night's football game showed Bradford's defensive superiority.

4. The Otmans collect hornet's nests.

5. For safety's sake, automobiles should have regular maintenance.

6. Unannounced drug testing may be the only way to keep public transportation safe.

7. Passengers ride helicopters between the two major airports.

8. Summer repairs on streets and highways are well underway in July.

9. Feeding backyard wildlife creates both advantages and disadvantages for the birds and animals.

10. Radio stations, as one form of media, influence voters through advertisements as well as news stories.

Exercise 1—Answers

1. Good. Writer will explain why.

2. Poor. An improvement: Although Bedford stone is beautiful, it has three disadvantages as a building material. Writer will explain the disadvantages.

3. Good. Writer will give examples why.

4. Poor. An improvement: Collecting hornet's nests is a challenging—and dangerous—hobby. Writer will explain how to collect—safely.

5. Good. Writer will explain why maintenance keeps autos safe.

6. Good. Writer will give details to support his opinion.

7. Poor. An improvement: Helicopter service between the two major airports has vastly improved flight connections. Writer will give details to show why.

8. Poor. An improvement: Summer repair jobs on streets and highways affect traffic flow. Writer will explain how to deal with the slowed traffic patterns.

9. Good. Writer will give details to show both advantages and disadvantages.

10. Good. Writer will tell how.

18
PARAGRAPH CONTENTS

Writers' thoughts are put together into units we call paragraphs—one thought, one paragraph. The GED essay requires that you be able to write well-developed paragraphs. Good paragraphs come about when the writer does four things:

1. uses specific details to support the statement of purpose,
2. puts the details in a logical order,
3. uses effective connecting words to show the logical order and to hold the paragraph together, and
4. stays on the subject

Let's study each of these four points.

PART 1: USING SPECIFIC DETAILS

You learned in Chapter 16 to use specific words. We looked, for instance, at the difference between such words as "building" and "seventy-five-story office." You practiced making vague words into specific words.

The same idea applies to details in a paragraph. The directions on the GED Test will often say, "Be specific," "Support your explanation with specific details and examples," or "State specific reasons and examples." Using specific ideas to explain your topic will make your essay sparkle. Compare the following two paragraphs that attempt to explain why the Tuesday Market may startle first-time visitors.

The Tuesday Farmers' Market

The Tuesday Farmers' Market may startle a first-time visitor. Vendors gather early and begin selling right away. They often buy from each other. All kinds of things are available for sale, some new and some old. All kinds of strange noises can be heard and all kinds of things can be seen. Even the people are a surprise. Yes, it's really a surprise to go to the Tuesday Farmers' Market if you've never been there before.

The statement of purpose is clear: The Tuesday Farmers' Market may startle a first-time visitor. The reader is ready for some specific details to help him be startled—or at least understand why first-time visitors would be startled. Unfortunately, in this paragraph, the reader is only told that he should be surprised at all kinds of unnamed things. The writer is telling, not showing.

Now let's look at the same topic with specific details:

The Tuesday Farmers' Market

The Tuesday Farmers' Market may startle a first-time visitor. Vendors gather by 5:00 A.M. every Tuesday, and by 5:30 the haggling begins. A bib-overalled, whiskered farmer bargains with a high school boy who has three pairs of pigeons for sale. They strike a deal, and the boy takes his cash to a stall selling fresh fried pork rinds and antiques. He buys the rinds, still warm. Nearby, Elvis Presley tunes squawk through a static-filled speaker, drowning out only temporarily the chickens squawking a few feet away. Across the aisle, a middle-aged woman displays old canning jars on the hood of her car, and a tobacco-chewing, black-aproned man puts new handles on old shovels, scythes, hoes, and axes. Rolls of carpet, jars of clear clover honey, loaves of banana bread, piles of clothes, coops of ducklings, pairs of beagles, boxes of hub caps, all seek bargain hunters. Country music on a car radio, bleating goats, yapping dogs, and cajoling vendors compete for attention. At the Tuesday Farmers' Market, cabbages, gooseberries, soap, vacuum sweepers, porch swings, socks, pocketknives, country hams, and sleeping bags go to the best haggler. For someone who's not been there before, it's a real surprise.

Now the reader has specific pictures in his mind! Notice that the writer has provided sounds as well as pictures as part of his description. Notice, too, that the second paragraph is longer than the first. Specific writing need not be long, and long paragraphs are not necessarily specific. On the other hand, if you must put a picture in your reader's mind, you can't do it with just a few splotches of paint. A good picture needs outline, color, detail, shading. Be sure your paragraph paints a good picture!

  Hint: Show, don't tell!

PART 2: PUTTING DETAILS IN ORDER

You must arrange the details in your paragraph so that your reader can follow them easily. Three kinds of arrangement are most common, and you will use the one that best fits the purpose of your paragraph. The three kinds of logical arrangements include time order, space order, and orders of importance. Let's look at each of the three kinds of arrangement.

Arrangement 1: Time Order

We use time order when we tell about something that happened or will happen over a period of time. Items are presented in the order in which they occur. Study the following sample paragraph that explains why the writer reaches Johnathan's house late:

We Were Long Lost, Friend

When we tried to reach Johnathan's house late last night, we faced a series of obstacles. First, some of the street signs were bent so that we couldn't read them. Then, after we made what we later learned were three wrong turns and came to a dead end, we decided we were lost. Since we didn't want to knock on anyone's door at

10:00 P.M., we drove south until we came to a twenty-four-hour market. We asked directions there and found we'd driven nearly thirty blocks the wrong way. After we retraced our steps, we found the right street, but it was barricaded as a result of some utility repairs. By the time we followed the detour seven blocks east and seven blocks back west, we finally reached Johnathan's house only to discover "no parking" signs on both sides of the street. As a result, we parked around the corner and walked to his door, knocking as we heard his clock chime ten-thirty.

This paragraph is written in time order. The events are told in the order in which they happened.

NOTE: Certain clue words help the reader follow the time, words like *when*, *first*, *then*, *after*, *since*, and *finally*. Such words are necessary to clarify the time order.

☞ Hint 1: Anytime your writing involves an explanation of something that has happened over a period of time, use time order to write about it.

☞ Hint 2: Anytime your writing involves an explanation of something your reader must do over a period of time—like repair his brakes, change his oil, prepare a gourmet dish—then use time order to write about it.

Arrangement 2: Space Order

We use space order when we tell about something according to the way it is arranged in space. The common orders are as follows:

left to right
right to left
top to bottom
bottom to top
front to back
back to front

Look at the following paragraph organized spatially, left to right.

The Storeroom

The storeroom was a jumble of boxes, buckets, and useless debris. On the far left, stacks of old newspapers and scrap cardboard reached nearly six feet high. Next to them, empty boxes sat inside one another at unstable angles. To the right of the boxes, hundreds of buckets, most empty, some tipped over, were heaped pyramid fashion nearly to the ceiling. On the far right, an assortment of broken boxes, buckets, broom handles, rags, and rusted cans littered the floor. Certainly the storeroom needed a good cleaning.

This paragraph is written in space order, or as the reader sees the subject in space. In this case, the writer takes the reader around the room from left to right.

NOTE: Special words, called connecting words, offer clues to the reader: *on the far left, on the right, next to.* Connecting words tell the reader where to look in his mind's eye. They help establish relationships between one idea and the next. Be sure to use these special words to help your reader follow your ideas. (See also "Using Good Connecting Words" later in this chapter.)

☞ Hint: Anytime your writing involves an explanation of the arrangement of something—like parts of a carburetor, components of a stereo, furniture in a room, houses on a block—use the spatial method of organization so that your reader can follow your explanation.

Arrangement 3: Orders of Importance

As the heading implies, this final method of arranging details offers more than one choice. Your paragraph details may be arranged by order of importance in one of three ways:

—most important detail to least important detail
—least important detail to most important detail
—next most important detail to most important detail

In order to make more sense of these, we need to look at each of them individually.

Choice 1: Most Important to Least Important

The outline for such organization should be rather obvious. The most important idea or detail comes first. The order could be listed something like this:

1. most important idea
2. second most important idea
3. third most important idea
4. fourth most important idea
5. least important idea

The following paragraph states and supports the writer's opinion that the circus world is one of extraordinary work and organization. The paragraph is organized from most important to least important.

Here Comes the Big Top!

From an adult point of view, a circus is an impressive operation. While children may think the trained animal acts and the trapeze artists are most impressive, adults are most awed by the mere logistics of getting all the equipment and people from one site to another. Once the entourage has reached its destination by truck, the massive operation of erecting an entire city overnight amazes outsiders. The operation calls not only for putting up the big top but also for providing seating for thousands. In addition, the circus people and animals must be housed and fed. Imagine providing enough food for hundreds of lions, tigers, bears, elephants, and hungry working people. Finally, the fact that hundreds of costumes are ready for the performance impresses anyone who has had to prepare a single costume for a simple amateur performance. The circus world must be one of extraordinary work and organization!

As you can see, the paragraph begins with the writer's most important idea and ends with his least important idea.

 Hint: A writer should use this organization when what he says first may be the only thing a reader reads. Newspaper writing usually follows such an organization. Often we read the first several paragraphs of a news item but fail to finish it. We know, however, that we have read the most important ideas.

Choice 2:   Least Important to Most Important

This second method of order of importance is more common than the first. In this case, the organization is exactly opposite of the first example we considered. The list of details would look something like this:

1. least important detail
2. fourth most important detail
3. third most important detail
4. second most important detail
5. most important detail

Following is the same sample paragraph, this time reorganized to follow this second method of order of importance. Note the difference.

Here Comes the Big Top!

From an adult point of view, a circus is an impressive operation. The fact that hundreds of costumes are ready for the performance impresses anyone who has had to prepare a single costume for an amateur performance. In addition, the circus people and animals must be housed and fed. Imagine providing enough food for hundreds of lions, tigers, bears, elephants, and hungry working people. More impressive, however, is the operation of erecting an entire city overnight. The operation calls not only for putting up the big top but also for providing seating for thousands. Most impressive of all, however, are the mere logistics of getting all the equipment and people from one site to another. The circus world must be one of extraordinary work and organization!

Note that while the organization changed, the clue words remain, telling the reader what to expect next: *in addition, more impressive, most impressive of all.*

 Hint 1: The writer should use this organization when he has no reason to believe his reader is antagonistic.

 Hint 2: At the same time, however, the writer wants to create an impact. He wants to hit his reader at the end with the really big idea. Reader will be impressed! Reader will be apt to remember the impression longer!

Choice 3:   Next Most Important to Most Important

Finally, let's look at the most common of the three orders of importance. (Even this section of your book is organized by order of importance!)

The list of details for next most important to most important organization should look something like this:

1. second most important detail
2. least important detail
3. fourth most important detail
4. third most important detail
5. most important detail

The same sample paragraph has been reorganized once again to follow this last method of organization by order of importance. Note the differences, and compare the paragraph with the outline list above.

Here Comes the Big Top!

From an adult point of view, a circus is an impressive operation. For instance, imagine the operation required in erecting an entire city overnight. Not only does the operation call for putting up the big top but also for providing seating for thousands. Even lesser details are impressive. The fact that hundreds of costumes are ready for the performance impresses anyone who has had to prepare a single costume for an amateur performance. In addition, the circus people and animals must be housed and fed. Imagine providing enough food for hundreds of lions, tigers, bears, elephants, and hungry working people. Most impressive of all, however, are the mere logistics of getting all the equipment and people from one site to another. The circus world must be one of extraordinary work and organization!

This final method of organization by order of importance still uses clue words to help the reader follow the pattern: *in addition, impressive, most impressive of all*.

☞ Hint 1: This is the most common organization using order of importance. Its impact is probably the reason for its frequent use.

☞ Hint 2: By saving the most important detail until last, the writer can make a big impact.

☞ Hint 3: By using the second most important detail first, the writer will have made a significant impact early as well. For this reason, such organization is especially helpful when the writer must convince the reader.

How you arrange the details in your paragraph, then, should be determined in large part by the subject of your paragraph.

 Remember: Certain subjects demand certain organization. Obviously, at times you will have two, perhaps three choices; but most of the time the subject and your purpose will dictate the organization.

PART 3: USING CONNECTING WORDS

Throughout this chapter, you have read references to "clue words" and an occasional mention of "connecting words." Now that we have talked about how to support a paragraph effectively, let's talk about ways to tie that support together. The ties help the reader get through all the details in an orderly fashion. They help him know when you're moving from one idea to another or from one step to another. The ties, or clue words, we will call *connecting words*. (Some books call them *transitions*.) Connecting words serve two purposes:

1. Used within the paragraph, connecting words tie sentences together. They serve as bridges from one sentence to another.
2. Used between paragraphs, connecting words tie paragraphs together, still serving as bridges, bigger bridges.

Below are listed some of the most common transitional words and phrases:

accordingly	consequently	in fact
also	after that	moreover
another	finally	last
first	at the same time	for instance
second	for example	nevertheless
next	otherwise	on the other hand
as a result	to begin with	similarly
at last	however	such
then	therefore	thus
but	and	

The words and phrases above serve as effective connecting words, but they are not the only means by which a writer achieves smooth writing. Other means of connecting ideas include the following:

—repetition of a word or phrase
—synonyms (words with the same meaning)
—demonstrative pronouns (this, that, these, those)
—pronoun reference
—repetition of an idea or topic

The following paragraph explains why picket fences remind the writer of his grandmother. The transitions are italicized and illustrate most of the means of tying supporting details together or providing clues to the reader.

Granny's Picket Fence

Seeing a white picket fence always makes me think about my grandmother. *She* had an immaculate *white picket fence* all the way around *her* yard. Every *slat* had a perfect inverted heart-shaped peak. *Those peaks* somehow made me think *Granny* was putting out *her* sign, because *she* literally opened *her heart* to all of *us* children, grandchildren, and neighbor children alike. *Whatever the case, that fence* was *her* pride and joy. Every time *she* cut the grass, *she* used a scissors to trim around every single *picket. Along the front walk,* where the round-top *picket* gate swung in to visitors, *Granny* painted a pineapple design on each of the *slats. That* was a *symbol* of hospitality, *she* said. The *fence* even told of *her* generosity, for *she* removed two *slats* in the side so *we children* could run from the neighbor's wading pool to *Granny's* tire swing without going all the way around front.

Connecting words abound! Without them, the reader is lost and the writer's message is clouded. Try your hand now at using effective connecting words.

PART 4: STAYING ON THE SUBJECT

Whether writing a paragraph or a long paper, a writer must stay on the subject. If he begins writing about hamburgers, he can't end up writing about catsup. The following paragraph attempts to explain how communities try to combat problems caused by pigeons. Unfortunately, the paragraph gets off the subject. As you read, see if you can find the point at which the writer begins getting off the subject.

Enjoying Pigeons, Not Problems
(a sample paragraph that gets off the subject)

Nearly every community tries to combat the problems pigeons create. While pigeons are docile and provide enjoyment in the parks for those who like to feed them peanuts and popcorn, they also create a health hazard where they most frequently roost. Some experts try simply to change the roosting place. Of course, that only causes the health hazard to relocate. In fact, one year, officials used chicken wire to close off a favorite roosting place; so the pigeons began roosting in our garage. They created not only a health hazard but a financial burden as well. We had to have the car repainted as a result of the frequent stains on the hood. In spite of that, I really like pigeons. In fact, we used to raise pigeons when I was a child. Some of them are quite beautiful, not only because of their colors but also because of the ruffs around their necks or the long feathers along their legs. Of course, these are special breeds. Other special breeds are racing pigeons and those that fly in groups called kits, tumbling and diving to the spectators' delight.

Obviously the writer lost track of his stated purpose, that communities try to combat the problems pigeons create. Where do you think he first loses unity? If you suspect the problem began when the pigeons moved into the garage, you're right! From that point on, the details no longer explain how communities battle the pigeon problem.

 Hint: As you write, keep your topic sentence in mind. Ask yourself this question:

Does every detail I am writing explain or support my statement of purpose?

PRACTICE

Exercise 1

Directions: Try your hand at making a vague paragraph into a specific one. Rewrite the paragraph below so that it creates a specific picture in your reader's mind.

Shoe Shopping

When Nan tried on nearly twenty pairs of shoes late Friday evening, the shoe salesman remained patient and helpful throughout the two hours. Nan told the clerk what kind of shoes she thought she wanted. The clerk brought out some for her to try on. Then Nan offered some additional explanation and the salesman brought out some more. After she tried some on, she changed her mind about what she wanted. So the salesman brought out still more shoes. Finally, after two hours, Nan decided on two pairs.

Exercise 1—Answers

Although any revision of the above paragraph will necessarily differ from any suggested revision, you can examine your revision on the basis of the following questions:

1. Does your revision include details about what Nan asked to see when she went into the shoe store?

2. Does the reader know what color, style, or size shoe Nan is looking for?

3. Does your revision tell the reader what the shoe salesman first brought out for Nan to try on? How many pairs, what color, what style, what size? Are they what Nan asked to try on?

4. Does your reader know how Nan reacted? Did she frown, scold, smile, try on all the shoes, just look and shake her head?

5. Does your reader see the shoe salesman's reactions? Does he smile, frown, remain expressionless, ask questions, make any encouraging remarks, agree with Nan?

6. When the salesman returns with more shoes, what does he bring? Are they different colors, different styles, different sizes? Does he ask any questions?

7. How many pairs of shoes does Nan try on? Does she walk in them, look in a mirror, wiggle her toes?

8. What is Nan like as a customer? Bold and bossy, kind and courteous, sharp and unkind, grouchy, concerned, pleasant?

9. We know the clerk remains patient throughout. Does your reader see him struggle but remain patient?

10. Finally, and most important of all, do you *show* your reader rather than tell him about Nan's episode in the shoe store?

Exercise 2

Directions: Put the following items in time order as if you were going to write a paragraph using the following statement of purpose:

Statement of Purpose: The potholes on Elm Street have become rapidly worse.

1. In early April, the first cracks began showing along the tire tracks in the westbound lane.

2. Last week, most drivers swerved out of the westbound lane and across the centerline to avoid the basketball-sized potholes.

3. Four weeks later, the first cracks began crumbling, leaving bits of gravel scattered across the street.

4. For some reason, the eastbound lane remains relatively smooth.

5. Now Elm Street is a one-lane street.

6. The baseball-sized holes soon became basketball-sized holes.

7. Then dozens more baseball-sized holes appeared.

8. The crumbling worsened by early May, and holes began to grow, first to baseball-sized holes.

9. By the middle of May, the individual holes were beginning to grow into whole colonies.

10. As drivers avoided the holes in the tire tracks, holes began appearing across the entire lane, small at first, but quickly catching up with the basketball-sized holes in the tracks.

Exercise 2—Answers

If you followed the clues within the sentences, you should have listed the sentences above in the following order:

Sentence 1 above will be 1 in chronological order.
Sentence 2 above will be 8 in chronological order.
Sentence 3 will be 2.
Sentence 4 will be 9.
Sentence 5 will be 10.
Sentence 6 will be 5.
Sentence 7 will be 4.
Sentence 8 will be 3.
Sentence 9 will be 6.
Sentence 10 will be 7.

Exercise 3

Directions: Rearrange the storeroom paragraph on page 154 so that the organization is right to left instead of left to right. When you finish, compare your paragraph to the one below. Don't cheat yourself; do your own before you look below.

Exercise 3—Answers

Your paragraph should look something like this:

The Storeroom

The storeroom was a jumble of boxes, buckets, and useless debris. On the far right, an assortment of broken boxes, buckets, broom handles, rags, and rusted cans littered the floor. To the left of that, hundreds of buckets, most empty, some tipped over, were heaped pyramid fashion nearly to the ceiling. Next to them, empty boxes sat inside one another at unstable angles. On the far left, stacks of old newspapers and scrap cardboard reached nearly six feet high. Certainly the storeroom needed a good cleaning.

Exercise 4

Directions: Determine which method of organization would be best for the following paragraphs. Choose time order (TO), space order (SO), or order of importance (OI). Answers follow below, but be sure you've made a decision before you consult the answer key.

1. an explanation of how to insulate a new house

2. an explanation of how to operate a drill press

3. a proposal supporting your opinion to eliminate billboards from the nation's highways

4. an explanation to a potential employer about why you are an excellent person for a particular job

5. the reasons for your building a fence around your property

6. the reasons why sunbathers should use sunscreen lotions

7. the reasons for using herbicides

8. a description of a farmer applying herbicides

9. the reasons we have tax laws

10. the process of implementing a new tax law

Exercise 4—Answers

You should have the following answers for the exercise above:

1. time order

2. time order

3. order of importance

4. order of importance

5. order of importance (or time order if a series of events has led to the building)

6. order of importance

7. order of importance

8. time order or space order (depending on whether the observer is with the farmer or watching from a distance)

9. order of importance

10. time order

Exercise 5

Directions: The paragraph below has no connecting words. Revise the paragraph to include effective connectors. A suggested revision follows below.

Rainy Afternoons

I like rainy afternoons. Rainy afternoons help me relax. I can read or nap. I can work on my hobby. My hobby is building radio-controlled gliders. I know I can soon fly the gliders. Thinking about flying them helps me relax. Flying gliders takes my mind off everything else. I really like rainy afternoons.

Exercise 5—Answers

The following paragraph offers a suggested revision for the exercise above. Obviously, your revision will be somewhat different from this one, but as long as you've used connecting words to provide good bridges between ideas, you have achieved the goal!

Rainy Afternoons

I like rainy afternoons because they help me relax. On those lazy afternoons when I can't be working outside, I can read or nap. In addition, I can work on my hobby, building radio-controlled gliders. Even during rainy times, I know I can soon take the glider out to fly, and just thinking about flying it helps me relax. I imagine myself steering it, seeking lifts to keep it slipping through the skies for an hour or more. The fantasizing, just like actually flying, takes my mind off everything else. As a result, rainy afternoons provide real relaxation!

Exercise 6

Directions: From the list of details below, mark out the ones which will not support the statement of purpose. These are the details which will cause the writer to get off the subject of his paragraph.

Statement of Purpose: Neon signs flash messages through the night in many forms and colors.

1. Some neon signs are multicolored.

2. I especially like the ones that look like script, spelling out words in color.

3. Computerized marquees are beginning to replace neon signs.

4. In daylight, neon signs seem lifeless and dull.

5. After driving in darkness, coming up on a neon sign can be really startling.

6. Those little tubes of light can take on the most amazing shapes and designs.

7. Some of the most fascinating neon signs are in Las Vegas.

8. Las Vegas billboards and marquees compete with each other not only in size but also in brilliance.

9. I was overwhelmed by the excessive lights that made late night as bright as noon.

10. Some neon signs use only the sky as their backdrop.

Exercise 6—Answers

Sentences 3, 4, 8, and 9 should be eliminated if the writer is to stay on the subject.

—In sentence 3, the writer should not talk about computerized marquees when his stated topic is neon signs.

—The statement of purpose refers to *night*, so sentence 4 should not be included since it refers to daylight.

—Sentence 8 should be omitted because details about billboards and marquees are not part of neon signs.

—In sentence 9, the writer should not discuss *all* lights, only neon lights.

19

PARAGRAPH ACCURACY

After you have written a clear statement of purpose and developed specific, organized supporting details with effective connecting words, you have ninety percent of the writing job done. GED essay evaluators, however, look for two other matters, and the GED writing skills questions address both of these matters as well:

correct verb tense
consistent point of view

This chapter shows you how to use both correctly.

PROBLEM 1: USING CORRECT VERB TENSE

A writer who uses verb tenses correctly helps his reader follow the paragraph's details. Tense, of course, shows time. Like time, tenses are relative. Their purpose is to show the time relationships among a series of events.

A. Using Simple Tenses

The three simple tenses, past, present, and future, are the easiest ways to show yesterday, today, and tomorrow. (See also Chapter 2, Step 2.)

EXAMPLE: (yesterday)   I *walked* home.   (past tense)
              (today)   I *walk* home.   (present tense)
              (tomorrow) I *will walk* home. (future tense)

NOTE: When we speak of using consistent verb tense, we simply mean that if you begin a piece of writing in past tense, continue the piece in past tense. Do not switch from past to present to future and back to past, unless, of course, you are intentionally *showing* a change in time.

B. Using Perfect Tenses

Even though we can easily recognize the simple yesterday, today, and tomorrow relationships, we must also recognize the difference between yesterday and the day before yesterday and the difference between tomorrow and next week. The perfect tenses allow us to be more exact—more perfect—in showing those time relationships:

EXAMPLE:
(yesterday)	I *walked* home.
(day before yesterday)	Until yesterday, I *had walked* home only once.
(between then and now)	I *have walked* three more miles since then.
(today)	Instead of driving, I *walk* home now.
(tomorrow)	I *will walk* home every day this next week.
(after tomorrow)	By next week this time, I *will have walked* twenty-five miles.

Without going into all the details, let's just say that the perfect tenses are a combination of some form of the verb "to have" (*have, has, had, will have*) plus the *-ed* form of the verb.

had walked

has walked, have walked

will have walked

Summarized, the perfect tenses carry these meanings:

had + verb = a past action completed prior to another past action.
Example: The potter *had completed* the demonstration before I arrived.

has or *have* + verb = a past action that continues into the present
Example: I *have planned* a party for this Saturday.

will have + verb = action that will be completed at a specified time in the future
Example: WIKY radio station *will have been* on the air fifty years next month.

C. Recognizing Progressive Form

Each of the six tenses can also appear in progressive form to show continuing action. Progressive form is characterized by the *-ing* ending.

EXAMPLE: The latest MGM release *is* now *showing* at the theater.

EXAMPLE: The line *was* already *forming* when we arrived.

EXAMPLE: The line *had been forming* for almost an hour before we arrived.

EXAMPLE: By next summer, I *will have been dieting* for a year.

D. Showing Time Relationships

We've all heard the cliche that today is the tomorrow you worried about yesterday. The cliche suggests how complicated it can be to show clear time relationships in your writing. The following example explains why the writer's vacation was exhausting. The paper illustrates the use of all six tenses, including some progressive forms. Marginal notes identify the changes in time.

New-Car Phobia

past tense (last summer)	Last summer's vacation *proved* really exhausting. Driving a brand
past tense (still last summer)	new car, I *worried* constantly that someone *would bang* his car door into mine, putting that first dent on the perfectly polished surface. As a result of
past tense (last summer)	my worry, I often *parked* blocks
past tense (last summer)	from where I *wanted* to visit so I
past tense (last summer)	*could park* away from menacing two-door cars. In addition, because of frequent rain showers, mud
past tense (last summer)	often *spattered* the car's lower body. In the evenings, then, even
perfect tense (to show an earlier action)	though exhaustion *had* already *hit*, I *made* certain I *found* a place to hand wash my car. After all, the
future tense (to show what will happen later)	dirt *will harm* the paint, and those car-wash places *will scratch*
past tense (last summer)	the finish. Or so I *thought*. Now
present tense (now)	that my car *is* a year old,
present tense (now)	however, and already *is* scratched
perfect tense (shows past action continuing into future)	and dented here and there, I *have been looking* forward to this summer's more
future tense (coming summer)	relaxing vacation. I *will park* as near
future tense (coming summer)	to my destination as I can. I *will*
future tense (coming summer)	*leave* the mud, or I *will drive* right into the nearest automated car wash! By next
perfect tense (shows action to be completed at specified time)	summer's end, I *will have enjoyed*—finally—a relaxing vacation.

 Remember: Consistency of verb tense is achieved not by using the same tense throughout a piece of writing, but rather by using the same point of reference and allowing all events to take their respective time relationships from that point.

PROBLEM 2: USING ONE POINT OF VIEW

A writer must use the same point of view throughout an essay. Point of view refers to the way the reader receives the message. If the point of view is first person, the reader learns about the writer's ideas through the writer's eyes. If the point of view is second person, the writer talks directly to the reader, giving commands or instructions. If the point of view is third person, both the reader and the writer are talking about a third party.

A. Identifying First-Person Point of View

Writers use the first-person point of view to tell about personal experiences or opinions. Certain words identify first person point of view:

I	me	my, mine
we	us	our, ours

Those personal pronouns in the first row are singular and those in the second row, plural. All show first-person point of view.

Look at these sample sentences written in first-person point of view:

EXAMPLE: During summer months, I usually try to get a part-time job working outdoors.
(The first-person pronoun *I* indicates point of view.)

EXAMPLE: Since my sister gave me that book, it is especially precious to me.
(The first-person pronouns *my* and *me* indicate point of view.)

EXAMPLE: Sometimes our neighborhood gets together for a block party, and we really learn to enjoy each other's company.
(The first-person pronouns *our* and *we* indicate point of view.)

B. Identifying Second-Person Point of View

Writers use second person point of view to give instructions, directions, or commands. Certain words indicate second person point of view:

you, your, yours

EXAMPLE: When you come in the house, take off your muddy boots.
(The second-person pronouns *you* and *your* show point of view.)

☞   Hint: Sometimes the second-person pronouns do not actually appear in print. Rather, they are understood.

EXAMPLE: Use extreme care when operating heavy machinery.
(second-person point of view for giving instructions; "you" is understood)

EXAMPLE: Take Exit 33 off the Broadway Expressway.
(second-person point of view for giving directions; "you" is understood)

EXAMPLE: Stop that noise!
(second-person point of view for issuing commands; "you" is understood)

C. Identifying Third-Person Point of View

Of the three points of view, experienced writers use third-person point of view most frequently. It is also the most versatile. The following personal pronouns indicate third-person point of view:

he	him	his
she	her	her, hers
it	it	its
they	them	their, theirs

In addition to these personal pronouns, however, third-person point of view results when writers use proper names or common nouns.

Hint: If the first- or second-person pronouns do not appear, the writing is in third-person point of view. (But remember, second-person pronouns can be implied.)

Consider these examples, all written in third-person point of view:

EXAMPLE: The head of a single-parent family must be well organized to succeed as both parent and wage earner.
(third-person point of view indicated by use of common noun *head*)

EXAMPLE: Sometimes Rodney drives like a maniac.
(third-person point of view indicated by the proper noun *Rodney*)

EXAMPLE: When high winds toss the garbage cans about, debris litters the neighborhood.
(third person indicated by common noun *debris*)

EXAMPLE: During lunch hour, they ate quietly.
(third person indicated by pronoun *they*)

D. Choosing Point of View

We have hinted throughout this section that one point of view may be more appropriate than another for a specific purpose. Following is a summary of those points:

1. Use first-person point of view to tell about personal experiences or to give a personal opinion.
2. Use second-person point of view to give instructions, directions, or commands.
3. Use third-person point of view for any writing purpose.
4. Use third-person point of view for formal writing.

By now you should have a fairly good grasp of what point of view is all about.

 Warning: Once you can identify the three points of view, you need only make sure that any given piece of writing uses the *same point of view throughout*.

In this chapter you have studied two kinds of consistencies, verb tense, and point of view. If you can apply these two principles to your own paragraphs, you will be well on the way to passing your GED essay with high scores.

PRACTICE

Exercise 1

Directions: The following paragraph does not use correct verb tense. Revise it so that tense is consistent and shows accurate time relationships.

The Money Battle

In last year's financial statement, the company indicates a serious financial loss, a problem which had since affected negotiations with the union. While company officials tried in the last three weeks to convince workers to accept a wage reduction, only yesterday had they agreed that the reduced wages would eventually be repaid. That news sparks positive reaction among union leaders. Now, if company officials would agree to accept the same terms for themselves, the union will be finding a basis for agreement.

Exercise 1—Answers

The following is a revision of the above paragraph. Verb tenses have been revised to show good time relationships.

The Money Battle

In last year's financial statement, the company *indicated* a serious financial loss, a problem which *has* since *affected* negotiations with the union. While company officials *have tried* in the last three weeks to convince workers to accept a wage reduction, only yesterday *did* they *agree* that the reduced wages *will* eventually *be repaid*. That news *sparked* positive reaction among union leaders. Now, if company officials *will agree* to accept the same terms for themselves, the union *will find* a basis for agreement.

Explanation:

indicated (Use past tense, in keeping with "last year's.")
has affected (Use perfect tense to show past action that continues into the present.)
have tried (Use perfect tense to show past action that continues into the present.)
did agree (Use past tense to show "yesterday.")
will be repaid (Use future tense to show future action.)
sparked (Use past tense to show "yesterday.")
will agree (Use future tense to show future action.)
will find (Use future tense to show future action.)

Exercise 2

Directions: The following paragraph is not consistent in its point of view. Revise it first so that it is written in first-person point of view, and then revise it so that it is in third-person point of view. Suggested revisions follow, but be sure to try your own version before you look.

Vacation Joy(less)

Long vacation trips can really wear you out. My family, for instance, usually plans to hop in the car at an outrageously early hour, drive 700 miles, fall asleep in some faceless motel, and repeat the whole procedure the next morning. You do that for seven or eight of the fourteen days and call it fun. After the end of the first day, though, I've had all I can take of arguments about when we'll stop for lunch, where we'll stop for lunch, or if we'll stop before lunch. You get bored with the ride, the same scenery sliding past at 65 miles an hour, the same ribbon of highway rolling ahead and behind. If a person wants to enjoy his vacation trip, he should walk more, see more, enjoy more, and certainly drive less.

Exercise 2—Answers

The following paragraph has been revised so that it maintains a consistent first-person point of view. Compare it with your own revision.

Vacation Joy(less)

Long vacation trips can really wear me out. My family, for instance, usually plans to hop in the car at an outrageously early hour, drive 700 miles, fall asleep in some faceless motel, and repeat the whole procedure the next morning. We do that for seven or eight of the fourteen days and call it fun. After the end of the first day, though, I've had all I can take of arguments about when we'll stop for lunch, where we'll stop for lunch, or if we'll stop before lunch. I get bored with the ride, the same scenery sliding past at 65 miles an hour, the same ribbon of highway rolling ahead and behind. If I want to enjoy my vacation trip, I should walk more, see more, enjoy more, and certainly drive less.

The following paragraph has been revised to maintain consistent third-person point of view. Compare this revision with your own.

Vacation Joy(less)

Long vacation trips can really wear a person out. Some families, for instance, usually plan to hop in the car at an outrageously early hour, drive 700 miles, fall asleep in some faceless motel, and repeat the whole procedure the next morning. They do that for seven or eight of the fourteen days and call it fun. After the end of the first day, though, some people have had all they can take of arguments about when they will stop for lunch, where they will stop for lunch, or if they will stop before lunch. They get bored with the ride, the same scenery sliding past at 65 miles an hour, the same ribbon of highway rolling ahead and behind. If they want to enjoy their vacation trip, they should walk more, see more, enjoy more, and certainly drive less.

20

CONCLUSION

Think about a television commercial you've seen recently. What were the last words, the lingering idea you were left to think about? The last words we see or hear gain a few extra seconds' thinking time before our brains dart off on another thought. As a result, final words earn the writer's special attention for the emphasis they have. A good conclusion forces the reader to deal with the writer's message and give it a last, lingering thought. A good writer wants to be sure his conclusion makes the best of the extra time.

METHODS OF CONCLUDING

The conclusion should complete the paragraph. Use one of these three methods to write an effective conclusion:

Method 1: The conclusion may restate the main idea without repeating it word for word.

EXAMPLE:

Statement of Purpose: Our long-awaited visit to Clingman's Dome, the highest point in Tennessee, brought nothing but disappointment.

Conclusion: As a result of the fog, rain, and wind, our visit to Clingman's Dome was disappointing.

Method 2: The conclusion may be a summary. It can help the reader pull the ideas together.

EXAMPLE:

Statement of Purpose: Evaluating one day's activity on the stock market demands a thorough understanding of how world affairs affect international economics.

Conclusion: Whether war, famine, political unrest, industrial accident, or scientific discovery, all of world affairs directly or indirectly affect the stock market.

Method 3: Sometimes, in a short paper, the conclusion may simply be the last statement.

EXAMPLE:

Statement of Purpose: The last day of vacation brought both relief and regret.

Conclusion: When the two weeks were over, I headed home, unpacked my luggage, and stored it in the attic for another fifty weeks.

The last-statement conclusion can be effective and leave the reader with a sense of completeness.

 Warning: A conclusion cannot contain a new idea that needs development of its own.

EXAMPLE:

Statement of Purpose: The last day of vacation brought both relief and regret.
Poor Conclusion: Now, two weeks later, I am enjoying my new exercise group.

The "new exercise group" has nothing to do with "the last day of vacation," so the reader is left wondering how it fits in the statement of purpose. If you add a new idea, the reader loses the sense of completeness. He's trying to figure out what this new idea has to do with the rest of your paragraph!

MODEL PARAGRAPH

The following paragraph explains why offensive and defensive football players see the game so differently. The paragraph illustrates an effective conclusion, one that gives a feeling of completeness without introducing new ideas.

Players' Jobs

Offensive and defensive football players' jobs differ significantly. For instance, the defensive end and the offensive end have opposite jobs. While the defensive end is supposed to prevent the running back from getting around him, the offensive end is trying in turn to block the defensive end. Basically, the offense is trying to score while the defense is trying to stop the scoring. To make these plays semi-automatic for a well-practiced football player, even the practice sessions for the defense and offense differ. In fact, often each group has its own coach, a specialist in the most successful tactics. For example, the defense drill to hit and hit hard, react and react quickly while the offense drill to build strength and to bodily move defensive players from the runner's path. Even though offense and defense play for the same team, the players themselves have a different understanding of how to play the game.

The conclusion is a restatement of the main idea (method 1), and it emphasizes the differences between the offense and defense by saying they "have a different understanding of how to play the game." The reader is left with a sense of completeness, knowing exactly what the writer has said.

As you write your own conclusion, choose the method which best suits the purpose of your paragraph.

PRACTICE

Exercise 1

Directions: Assume you have developed a paragraph supporting each of the following statements of purpose. Now, write a concluding sentence for each. Of course, answers will vary widely, but some possible answers follow.

1. Refinishing the kitchen cabinets seemed at first an insurmountable task.

2. My first driving experience in big-city traffic nearly caused me to resign from ever driving again.

3. Uncle Earl has developed a foolproof technique for locating the elusive largemouth bass.

4. Hiking boots provide necessary protection for anyone tramping through back country.

5. Cross-country skiers experience the outdoors in a dimension the rest of us cannot share.

6. White wicker furniture combined with abundant green plants transformed the drab room into a sunny retreat.

7. Our neighbor, who sometimes seems eccentric, adheres to a strict daily routine.

8. Weekends offer a welcome respite from workday routines.

9. Contractors met unanticipated obstacles as they struggled to complete the apartment complex on schedule.

10. Community environmentalists fear the impact on clean air by the proposed paper mill.

Exercise 1—Answers

The following statements will make suitable conclusions for the corresponding statements of purpose above. Your answers will, of course, vary, but as long as you've used one of the three methods for developing a conclusion, no doubt yours will also be acceptable.

1. So, when the job was done, we realized the step-by-step process hadn't been so difficult after all.

2. As a result of such harrowing experiences, I almost refused to get behind the wheel again.

3. Uncle Earl's technique will certainly reap big catches for anyone who uses it.

4. Without hiking boots, then, the back country adventurer risks more than he can afford to risk—a way back out.

5. No other mode of transportation can afford such a close-up look at the great outdoors.

6. Now we spend many pleasure-filled hours in a peaceful, restful atmosphere.

7. By the end of the day, our eccentric has exhausted himself from the routine.

8. Ah, what wonderful things, weekends!

9. With an added complication at every turn, contractors will be lucky to finish on schedule.

10. As a result, the community watchdogs will have ample support in fighting their battle.

CHECKLIST FOR WRITING POWERFUL PARAGRAPHS

Use the following checklist to evaluate your own paragraphs. You should be able to answer "yes" to each of these questions.

		YES	NO
1.	Have I written a good statement of purpose?	☐	☐
2.	Have I used specific details to support the statement of purpose?	☐	☐
3.	Have I arranged the details in logical order?	☐	☐
4.	Have I included only details which support the statement of purpose? In other words, have I avoided getting off the subject?	☐	☐
5.	Have I used good connecting words?	☐	☐
6.	Have I used the right verb tenses?	☐	☐
7.	Have I used the same point of view throughout?	☐	☐
8.	Have I selected the most appropriate point of view?	☐	☐
9.	Have I written an effective conclusion?	☐	☐
10.	Have I written effective, powerful, complete sentences?	☐	☐
11.	Have I used good sentence variety?	☐	☐
12.	Have I used specific, concise words?	☐	☐
13.	Have I checked for grammar, mechanics, and usage?	☐	☐
14.	Have I checked spelling?	☐	☐

VII

FOUR KINDS OF ESSAYS

21

EXPLAINING HOW

One of the four general kinds of topics you may be asked to write about on the GED essay test is one that asks you to explain how. An essay that explains how may, for instance, tell about the steps followed in landing a job or the steps needed to keep within a monthly budget.

The single most important part of writing a how-to paper is *organization*. If the steps for getting the task done are not in step-by-step order, the reader will be unable to follow them.

Here's how to write a paper that explains how.

ORGANIZATION

A paper that explains how will probably use the following general plan:

• The paper will begin with a statement of purpose that names the process and says something about the task—how easy or how difficult, how simple or how time-consuming.

> EXAMPLE: Packing a canoe for a trip through white water calls for certain precautions.
> (The writer will explain how to pack the canoe.)
> EXAMPLE: Arranging for a surprise birthday party requires careful planning.
> (The writer will explain the steps showing how to plan a surprise birthday party.)

• The opening statement also shows the importance of the subject, telling why anyone would want to know how to do this.

> EXAMPLE: Knowing how to shop wisely can save dollars for the comparison shopper.
> (explaining how to do comparison shopping)
> EXAMPLE: If you sign your name on the wrong dotted line, you may end up renting an apartment for longer than you want.
> (explaining how to understand rental leases)

• The paper will be organized in time order. (See Chapter 18, Part 2.) The paper must show step-by-step how to do whatever it is that you are explaining: do this first, then do this, etc.

• Connecting words should appear frequently. They help the reader follow the time order. Common how-to connecting words include the following:

first	next	at this time
second	then	following this
third	at this time	after
now	afterward	soon
thus	in addition	therefore
furthermore	hence	similarly
at this point	after this	

• The conclusion should summarize and restate the result of step-by-step procedure.

MODEL

The following example is a well written how-to paper. Study the notes in the margins as you read.

How to Eat Peas—Politely

subject named
opening statement shows
   importance to reader (to
   be polite)
third-person point of
   view established

Eating peas in polite company can be a real test of agility. Courtesy denies the opportunity to mash the peas and scoop them up with a fork. Courtesy also disallows using a spoon to eat peas. Attempting to spear peas on the tines of the fork usually results in those little green spheres skittering across the plate into one's lap—or worse yet, onto a fellow diner's lap. A few simple steps will allow the polite diner to eat peas in relative comfort.

statement of purpose
   referring to "simple"
   steps
connecting word introducing
   time order

First, the peas must reside next to a more solid food, like mashed potatoes or meatloaf. When the diner has the opportunity to serve the peas himself, he will, of course, want to situate them on his plate to his advantage. If the dinner plate is presented already filled, however, the diner has the tedious job of relocating the peas without appearing rude.

connecting words showing
   continuing steps

Once the peas are situated next to a more solid food, however, the next steps are easy. By placing the fork beside the peas, tines against the

third-person point of view
used throughout

connecting word showing
final step

connecting word signaling
the conclusion
conclusion offers indirect
challenge to reader

plate, the diner merely shoves the fork under the peas. The solid food will prevent the peas from rolling with the fork. Finally, as one nears the end of his meal, he must be certain to leave sufficient solid food until the last of the rolling vegetables are safely hoisted away. In this manner, the polite diner wins the battle with peas without using his fingers or a dinner roll as a pusher.

PRACTICE

Directions: To practice your own how-to writing, select a topic from those listed below, or choose your own topic. When you finish writing, use the checklist that follows to think through your paper.

Selected Topics

—how to plan a vacation
—how to start a car on a cold morning
—how to pick a winning movie
—how to choose a restaurant/motel/vacation spot
—how to choose a restaurant/motel/vacation spot for children
—how to buy a used car
—how to buy the perfect birthday/Christmas/anniversary/wedding gift
—how to improve your golf game/bridge game/tennis game
—how to drive safely in heavy traffic
—how to win friends/enemies

CHECKLIST FOR WRITING A PAPER THAT EXPLAINS HOW

Use the following checklist to judge your paper. You should be able to answer "yes" to these questions.

		YES	NO
1.	Does my paper include a statement that names the subject and suggests the ease or care with which the process can be completed?	☐	☐
2.	Have I shown the importance of the subject?	☐	☐
3.	Have I used plenty of specific details, clearly explaining each step in the process?	☐	☐
4.	Have I organized the paper in time order?	☐	☐
5.	Have I used clear connecting words to help establish the time order?	☐	☐
6.	Have I omitted ideas not directly related to my topic?	☐	☐
7.	Have I used the right verb tenses, especially as I developed my paper by time order?	☐	☐
8.	Have I maintained consistent point of view?	☐	☐
9.	Does my conclusion summarize, restate the result of the process, and challenge the reader?	☐	☐
10.	Have I used good, effective, complete sentences?	☐	☐
11.	Have I used good sentence variety?	☐	☐
12.	Have I used specific, concise words?	☐	☐
13.	Have I used good grammar and accurate mechanics and usage?	☐	☐
14.	Have I checked spelling?	☐	☐

22

EXPLAINING WHY

We often ask "why?" Why am I grumpy after lunch? Why won't the car start? Why am I so short of money this month? Because explaining why is such a part of daily life, the GED essay topic may ask you to "Explain why and support your explanation with examples and specific details."

The following samples illustrate what a writer does when he explains why:

Sentence 1: The severe snow and ice storm caused especially serious problems in rural areas.
(The writer will explain why the problems were so serious: power failures, impassible roads, homes without heat or water, livestock stranded without food.)

Sentence 2: The severe snow and ice storm resulted when the low-pressure storm system joined moisture from the Gulf.
(The writer, who must be familiar with the science of weather forecasting, will explain why the storm occurred.)

> **NOTE:** Explaining why can deal with causes: why something happened. It can also deal with results: why something is the way it is.

ORGANIZATION

A paper that explains why usually uses the following organization:

• The paper should begin with an attention-getter that establishes the importance of the subject.
• The paper should include a statement of purpose. (See Chapter 17.)

EXAMPLE: In order to survive, workers in today's labor force must learn to deal with stress.
(The writer will explain the reasons why workers must learn to deal with stress.)

EXAMPLE: The car failed to start because of a series of weather related events.
(The writer will explain the reasons why the weather caused the car not to start.)

• In a paper that explains why, the statement of purpose is followed by specific examples and specific details. (See Chapter 18.)

EXAMPLE: Workers must learn to deal with stress because they face stress on a daily basis.

Detail 1: face stress keeping job (lay-offs, strikes, plant closings, cutbacks)

Detail 2: face stress completing work (daily and weekly deadlines, work output per hour, meeting rates)

Detail 3: face stress in labor-management relations (union policy vs. employee demands, demanding boss, personal conflicts)

EXAMPLE: Weather related events caused car not to start.

Detail 1: sub-zero cold followed by very warm temperatures

Detail 2: change brought condensation

Detail 3: moisture in ignition system

- The supporting details may be organized in either of two patterns: time order or order of importance. (See Chapter 18, Part 2.)

 Hint: Decide on your plan of organization before you begin writing. Jot down the ideas you want to include and decide whether time order works better than an order of importance or vice versa.

For instance, in the first example above, order of importance will work best: some kinds of stress are more difficult to deal with than others. In the second example, however, time order is essential. The writer must explain the series of events which resulted in the car not starting.

- Strong connecting words must tie together details and show the reader time relationships and cause-effect relationships. Some useful transitions include *therefore, hence, consequently, accordingly, as a result, for this reason, thus,* and *so.* (See Chapter 18, Part 3.)
- The conclusion should relate directly to the statement of purpose and tie together the logical steps presented. (See Chapter 20.)

MODELS

The following paragraphs explain why. Study them before you write your own.

Sun Worshipping

introductory statement

> Everywhere, from beaches to backyards, sun worshippers lie in the blazing heat soaking up rays.

attention-getter that shows impact of subject

> The resulting business in suntan lotions, sunscreens, beach towels, sunglasses, skin conditioners, hair conditioners, and medical bills for skin-cancer treatments

statement of purpose (in form of question)

> adds up to big dollars. What causes apparently sane people to

connecting word and first cause (reason why)

details supporting first reason why

connecting word and second reason why
specific details supporting second reason why

connecting words showing relationship of groups one and two to group three
third reason why

specific details supporting third cause

conclusion in two statements (both referring to statement of purpose and introduction and both suggesting writer's attitude about "logic" of reasons why)
"golden" teases, makes final statement

subject themselves to such discomfort and risk? First, some folks actually enjoy the sweltering experience. They like the feel of oil all over their bodies and the sun oozing sweat out of their every pore. They must see it as a kind of cleansing act that pays penance for whatever wrongs they have done. "Sweating it out" becomes almost heroic. Other folks, however, lie under Old Sol out of an apparent sense of duty. They don't like the oil-and-sand mixture on their skins, and they don't like to sweat. On the other hand, however, since all their friends soak in the sun, peer pressure indicates they, too, must soak in the sun. How could they make up an acceptable excuse not to join in? Finally, there are the folks who neither enjoy the sun nor feel a sense of duty to join the worshippers. They are the ones who think a tan is the absolute epitome of good grooming. A tan, they are convinced, makes them gorgeous; it attracts the opposite sex; it earns them better jobs; it authorizes them to be better than anyone else who doesn't have an equally golden tan. So they believe. The non-sun worshipper looks with raised eyebrows at any of these golden bodied reasons, questioning the sanity and pointing to statistics about causes of skin cancer. On the other hand, stockholders in suntan-lotion companies cheer the golden business.

The model above explains why a sunbather lies in the sun. The writer considers three possible reasons why people sunbathe.

The following model illustrates another kind of reason why. It shows why a situation brings certain results. Notice that the general principles and methods of organization are the same. The writer merely approaches the situation from a different direction, explaining why things are as they are. It's the difference between cause and effect. (Note: You have read other short models throughout the text that explain why. You may wish to review them as well.)

Sun Worshippers, Beware!

introductory statement	Sun worshippers embrace the blazing rays and welcome the
statement of purpose showing paper will tell why sun-bathing is bad.	golden tan. They usually forget, however, the other less desirable effects of sunbathing. First, the
connecting word introducing first effect	general discomfort from lying in the broiling heat must have some
organization in order of importance, least to most	consideration. Sweat oozes from every pore, lotions with their heavy oily texture block the
details to explain first reason why	pores; and sand or grass mixes with the lotion to produce an on-skin sandpaper. Although these
connecting words	discomforts are only temporary,
second part of first reason why	others may be more lasting. Folks who lie out too long too soon
details explaining "more lasting"	experience painful sunburns, soon followed by itching and uncomfortable peeling. Certainly the splotches that result aren't very attractive, but, of course, that discomfort is only emotional.
connecting words showing order of importance and naming second reason why	Second, and more important, however, is the productive time a sunbather loses. If he spends only an hour a day seeking a
example supporting second reason why	golden tan, a sunbather loses seven hours a week, the equivalent of a full working day.
challenge to the reader	Imagine the gain if such hours were spent doing something either personally or socially productive!
connecting word showing relationship of reasons one and two to three	Finally, dismissing the personal discomfort and the loss of productive time, the sunbather assumes a serious risk of physical
third reason why	problems. The problems may be as
series of examples supporting third reason why	simple as nausea or headache from too much heat. They may be more complicated such as an allergy to direct sun. Ultimately, the
connecting word showing order of importance	problems can be as serious as cancer. In fact, research is
connecting word and additional example of third reason why	beginning to make many serious-minded people less and less interested in Old Sol's dangerous
connecting word and summary of ideas in concluding statement leaving reader with serious thought	rays. In short, the effects from sunbathing range from general, short-termed discomfort to specific, long-termed physical problems, potentially fatal.

PRACTICE

Directions: To practice writing a paper explaining why, select a topic from those listed below, or choose your own topic. Write your paper. Then, use the checklist that follows to check your paragraph.

Suggested Topics

—why I landed the job

—why the accident occurred

—why I/someone was late for work/appointment/class

—why an industry leaves/closes/cuts back/lays off

—why we should eat/exercise properly

—what brings about failure/success in class/career/society

—why I/others respond to a specific advertising/political campaign

—what caused me to buy a certain car

—what causes me to shop at a certain shop/dine at a certain restaurant

—what causes me/someone to be rude/especially courteous/angry

CHECKLIST FOR WRITING A PAPER THAT EXPLAINS WHY

Use the following checklist to judge your paper that explains why. You should be able to answer "yes" to each of these questions.

		YES	NO
1.	Have I started with a statement of purpose?	☐	☐
2.	Have I included specific examples and details to support my reasons?	☐	☐
3.	Are my specific examples and details logical?	☐	☐
4.	Have I anticipated my readers' probable questions?	☐	☐
5.	Have I arranged the details of my paper either in time order or by some order of importance?	☐	☐
6.	Have I omitted ideas not directly related to my topic sentence?	☐	☐
7.	Have I used good connecting words?	☐	☐
8.	Have I used the right verb tenses?	☐	☐
9.	Have I used the same point of view throughout?	☐	☐
10.	Does my conclusion refer to the topic and tie together the logical steps in the paper?	☐	☐
11.	Have I written effective, powerful, complete sentences?	☐	☐
12.	Have I used specific, concise words?	☐	☐
13.	Have I used good grammar, mechanics, and usage?	☐	☐
14.	Have I spelled all the words correctly?	☐	☐

23

STATING AND SUPPORTING AN OPINION

Everybody has opinions, but being able to state and support those opinions so that others understand them is the mark of an educated person. As a result, one of the four general kinds of essay topics on the GED test asks you to do just that: state and support an opinion. Being able to do so shows first that you can think clearly and second that you can communicate effectively— both important for success on the GED test. Here's how to write an effective opinion paper.

ORGANIZATION

The following pattern of organization is typical of an opinion paper:

- The opinion paper usually begins with a statement of purpose. (See Chapter 17.)
- The supporting details must emphasize reasons for your opinion. Why do you think as you do? What examples can you give that help your reader understand why you think as you do?

NOTE: The GED essay response directions will usually say, "Be specific. Give reasons and examples." If you do not, you will surely receive a low score.

☞ Hint 1: Phrases like *in my opinion* or *I believe* need not appear in an opinion paper. Your name appears on the paper, and that is sufficient to let the reader know whose opinion he is reading. Of course, if you express an opinion other than your own, it should be preceded by phrases like *in the opinion of some* or *some people believe that* to avoid confusing your reader.

☞ Hint 2: If you need to soften certain points or limit their impact, you can use qualifying words like *in some cases*, *in most situations*, *occasionally*, *sometimes*, *perhaps*, *may*, and *probably*.

- The paper should maintain a consistent point of view. (See Chapter 19, Problem 2.)
- Opinion papers are usually organized by order of importance. (See Chapter 18, Part 2.)

Hint: The most effective organization plan for an opinion essay is the order of importance that uses the following pattern:

Detail one:	second most important
Detail two:	least important
Detail three:	fourth most important
Detail four:	third most important
Detail five:	most important

Because the opinion paper may be read by someone who disagrees with your point of view, the paper should build to its most important detail.

- Good connecting words help the reader follow the reasoning in an opinion paper. (See Chapter 18, Part 3.) Some typical connecting words for an opinion paper include *first, second, finally, on the one hand, on the other hand, in addition, as a result,* and *another reason.*
- The conclusion should help the reader understand your stated opinion.

MODEL

The following model shows what a good opinion paper should look like.

Do It Yourself: Fad or Fundamental?

introductory statement
statement of purpose

"Making your own" has become the thing to do. Whether it's making clothes, baking bread, making yogurt, or building a car, the do-it-yourself fad appears destined to lose its fad status and become the mark of the well-rounded

first point in order of
  importance

specific examples

person. Originally, the do-it-yourselfers claimed their purpose was to save dollars. Save dollars they did. By building his own custom fishing rod, one do-it-yourselfer had a rod valued at

third-person point of
  view used throughout

$150 that he'd made for less than $50. Another made her own suit for less that $40, one she would have paid well over $100 for in a

connecting word to second
  point

local department store. While some do-it-yourselfers still talk about dollars saved, others are now more apt to point out the

second reason for opinion
specific example to support
  second reason

purity or quality of the homemade product. They can boast of vegetables organically grown and home-canned and home-baked

third-person point of view;
  no reference to "my
  opinion" or "I think"

products with no additives and no preservatives. The man who builds his own car boasts of enduring

connecting word showing relationship of first two points to third point

connecting word showing "most important"

third reason for opinion

details explaining third reason

details explaining third reason

logical steps following

logical steps leading to conclusion

conclusion restating topic sentence

quality that will keep his car on the road years longer than those mass-produced. Even with the dollars saved and the purity and quality gained, perhaps the most important purpose in "making your own," however, is the resulting self-satisfaction. The mass-production society allows little room for self-satisfaction in the daily job. It's difficult at the end of a workday to see what's been accomplished, to point to a product of the day's labor. Then, at home, when the loaf of whole-wheat bread comes out of the oven, there, at last, is a product of one's labor, a product to touch, smell, taste, and enjoy. It feels good. So begins the do-it-yourself concept. If making bread brings about such good feelings, maybe growing herbs will feel good, too. And then maybe growing a small vegetable garden will feel even better. As the good feelings intensify and assume a kind of ripple effect, they will guarantee a continuing "make your own" attitude. The fad idea will no doubt disappear and be replaced by a practiced part of personal development.

PRACTICE

Directions: After studying the model paper above, you should be able to write your own opinion paper. To practice, choose from the suggested topics below or select your own. Then, when you've finished your paper, use the following list to check your paper.

Suggested Topics

It is my opinion that . . .

—everyone should have flu shots.

—not everyone should vote.

—some people have a valid reason for not getting a high school diploma.

—everyone should spend an hour each month helping the community clean up litter.

—everyone should read a daily newspaper instead of watching the news on television.

—a parent can be a son's/daughter's best buddy.

—the media influence voter reaction.

—women are effective wage earners.

—men make good househusbands as well as women make good housewives.

—computers can't replace the work force.

CHECKLIST FOR WRITING AN OPINION PAPER

Use the following checklist to think through your own opinion paper. You should be able to answer yes to each of these questions.

		YES	NO
1.	Have I written an effective statement of purpose?	☐	☐
2.	Have I used specific details to explain why I hold my opinion?	☐	☐
3.	Do the details take into consideration possible reader apathy or opposition?	☐	☐
4.	Have I used effective organization, probably one of the orders of importance?	☐	☐
5.	Have I used good connecting words?	☐	☐
6.	Have I omitted unnecessary phrases like "I believe" or "in my opinion"?	☐	☐
7.	Have I softened certain points or limited their impact with qualifying words?	☐	☐
8.	Have I stayed on the subject?	☐	☐
9.	Have I used the right verb tenses?	☐	☐
10.	Have I used the same point of view throughout?	☐	☐
11.	Have I written an effective conclusion that helps the reader understand my stated opinion?	☐	☐
12.	Have I used effective, powerful, complete sentences?	☐	☐
11.	Have I used good sentence variety?	☐	☐
13.	Have I used specific, concise words?	☐	☐
14.	Have I checked grammar, mechanics, and usage?	☐	☐
15.	Have I checked spelling?	☐	☐

24

SHOWING ADVANTAGES AND DISADVANTAGES

Sometimes the GED essay topic will ask you to talk about the advantages (the good points) and the disadvantages (the bad points) about some topic. Such an essay will obviously have two parts: one part will talk about all the advantages; another part will talk about all the disadvantages. But be sure to read the directions carefully. The directions may ask that you address only advantages *or* disadvantages—not both. In either case, here is the general plan for writing a paper that discusses advantages and/or disadvantages.

ORGANIZATION

The advantage-disadvantage paper will usually follow this plan:

- The paper begins with a statement of purpose that tells the reader that you will be talking about two points: advantages and disadvantages.

EXAMPLE: Commuting an hour or more to work each day has advantages and disadvantages. (We know the writer will talk about both the good and the bad, but we have no idea of the specifics.)

☞   Hint 1: You can write a better statement of purpose that does not repeat the words *advantages and disadvantages*.

EXAMPLE: Commuting an hour or more to work each day gives me both time to myself and added frustrations. (We know now that the writer sees "time to self" as an advantage, perhaps to read, finish up office reports, or think through what needs to be done at home or at work. But he sees "added frustrations" as disadvantages, perhaps because of the expense of commuting or the stress of fighting traffic or meeting bus, subway, or train schedules.)

☞   Hint 2: If the directions ask that you write about only advantages *or* disadvantages, your statement of purpose must clearly state which you will be discussing.

EXAMPLE: Commuting an hour or more to work each day adds nothing but frustration.
(The writer will show the disadvantages of the long commute.)

• The statement of purpose will be followed first by details about either all of the advantages or all of the disadvantages. Then will follow the details about the other.

☞ Hint 1: To decide whether to discuss advantages or disadvantages first, decide which you think are more important. For instance, if you think the advantages outweigh the disadvantages, talk about disadvantages *first*. Then you can end with your stronger point.

Example Topic:	Driving a Small Car
Advantages:	good gas mileage
	fits in small parking spaces
	maneuvers well in traffic
	quick acceleration, peppy
	fits in garage with room for more
	costs less to buy
Disadvantages:	only four people can ride
	trunk too small (groceries, luggage)
	expensive maintenance
	noisy
	insufficient power for air conditioner

Except for creature comforts (crowding, noisy, hot), the listed advantages seem to outweigh the disadvantages. So the plan may look like this:

Statement of Purpose:	Although the creature comforts are limited in a small car, the advantages make it a wise choice.
Disadvantages:	creature comforts (crowding, noisy, hot)
	expensive maintenance
Advantages:	inexpensive to buy, insure, and drive
	handles well in traffic and in parking
	fits in garage with room for more

☞ Hint 2: Of course, if you are writing only about advantages *or* disadvantages, rather than both, then you will have only one part to your paper. Then you need only organize the details by some order of importance. (See below.)

• The details in each part should be organized by some order of importance. (See Chapter 18, Part 2.) The best two choices:

Choice 1: least important to most important
Choice 2: second most important to most important

• The paper will need strong connecting words to help readers follow your points.

☞ Hint 1: Use good connecting words to tie together all the advantages. Use words and phrases like *one big advantage, another advantage, perhaps not as important but worth mentioning, the biggest advantage, yet another, finally.*

☞ Hint 2: Use good connecting words to tie together all the disadvantages. Use words and phrases like *one major disadvantage, another disadvantage, perhaps less important but still worth considering, the biggest disadvantage, yet another, finally.*

☞ Hint 3: Use a connecting *sentence* to tell your reader when you are changing from advantages to disadvantages or vice versa. One of the following may be useful:

EXAMPLES:

—While the advantages are numerous, the disadvantages are even more numerous.
—While the disadvantages may seem overwhelming, the advantages offer definite consideration.
—Even though the advantages sound beneficial, the disadvantages cause serious problems.
—Even though the disadvantages seem serious, the advantages are worth examining.

• The conclusion should acknowledge both advantages and disadvantages but reach a conclusion about which is the better choice.

Example Conclusion: Even though it comes with a few creature discomforts, the small car brings two other important comforts: driving and paying the expense of driving.

Study the following model to see how a completed paper should look.

MODEL

Advantages and Disadvantages of Small-Town Living

statement of purpose naming three disadvantages and two advantages, in order of importance
writer uses order to imply advantages more important than disadvantages
connecting words, disadvantages to be discussed first
first disadvantage, least important
supporting details to explain first disadvantage

Small-town living cannot offer the variety of cultural events, comparison shopping, and job opportunities that city living offers, but it can guarantee a slower pace and the support of friendly neighbors.

Consider first what small-town living cannot offer. Those who enjoy the theater and concerts face a disadvantage living in small towns. A civic group may put on an amateur production, or the high-school orchestra may have a spring recital, but small-town residents must travel to the cities to see equity actors or actresses or hear fine

connecting words to introduce second disadvantage,
   second most important
second disadvantage
supporting details to explain
   second disadvantage

connecting words to introduce third disadvantage,
   most important
specific details to explain
   reasons why about third
   disadvantage

connecting sentences to
   introduce second part,
   about advantages
direct answers to three
   disadvantages

connecting words to introduce first advantage
first advantage
specific examples to explain
   first advantage

connecting words to introduce second advantage

philharmonic concerts. Another disadvantage results from the relatively few businesses in small towns. There is no comparison shopping. When only one store sells boots, only one sells draperies, and only one sells carpet and other floor coverings, customers don't "shop around"; they either buy or not. Some small towns, however, have two grocers, and they may advertise the price of ground beef or Coca Cola to show a competitive spirit. The biggest disadvantage to small-town living, however, is the lack of job opportunities. Even someone who manages to find a job in one of the few businesses has little opportunity for advancement. Since almost all small-town businesses are family owned, the family takes care of its own. So unless a person is already part of a family-owned business or plans to open his or her own business, the chances are slim for successful employment.

So why live in a small town? Those who live there say that the advantages outweigh the disadvantages. Small-town folks say they can always drive to the city for cultural events or a shopping spree. And they can commute to a job. They are willing to make the drive first of all because of the quieter, slower pace. Small-town traffic is minimal. Traffic jams are something small-town folks only read about or see on television. Rarely do sirens interrupt a quiet dinner or an evening's rest. No one hurries anywhere. A driver may stop along the street to chat with a neighbor-pedestrian, and no impatient honks shorten the friendly greeting. Even though some folks commute to a job in a larger city, they look forward to returning to the friendly community they call home. That may be the biggest advantage:

second advantage

examples to explain second
  advantage

more examples to explain
  second advantage

still more examples to
  explain second advantage

connecting words to introduce
  conclusion
conclusion emphasizes
  advantages, obviously
  writer's preference

everyone knows everyone else, and help is always part of the neighborliness. Weather permitting, windows and doors are open, day and night. Neighbors watch each other's pets, water each other's flowers and gardens, and take in each other's mail during vacations. And when someone needs a baby-sitter, someone always watches—free. Neighbors visit from adjoining gardens, chatting about children and grandchildren, lack of rain, the price of gasoline, or last night's full moon. And after a snowstorm, whoever has his grader blade on his tractor first cleans the neighborhood driveways. In short, the advantages of small-town living reduce stress and create a kind of life that makes the going easy—slow and easy.

PRACTICE

Directions: Write your own advantage-disadvantage paper using one of the topics below or a topic of your own. After you finish writing, use the checklist that follows to think through your paper.

Discuss the advantages and disadvantages of

—living alone

—working nights

—being the age you are

—owning a car

—renting a house/apartment/furniture/appliances

—buying a used/new car

—belonging to a union

—adopting a child/children

—owning a cat/dog/bird/other pet

—having painted/papered walls

CHECKLIST FOR AN ADVANTAGES-DISADVANTAGES PAPER

	YES	NO
1. Have I written an effective statement of purpose?	☐	☐
2. Have I put all the advantages together and all the disadvantages together?	☐	☐
3. Have I put last the part (advantages or disadvantages) that I think is more important?	☐	☐
4. Have I arranged the details in order of importance, probably with the most important last?	☐	☐
5. Have I used good connecting words to tie together the details about advantages and disadvantages?	☐	☐
6. Have I used a good connecting sentence (or sentences) to move from advantages to disadvantages?	☐	☐
7. Have I stayed on the subject?	☐	☐
8. Have I used the right verb tenses?	☐	☐
9. Have I used the same point of view throughout?	☐	☐
10. Have I included an effective conclusion that says whether advantages outweigh disadvantages or vice versa?	☐	☐
11. Have I used effective, powerful, complete sentences?	☐	☐
12. Have I used good sentence variety?	☐	☐
13. Have I used specific, concise words?	☐	☐
14. Have I checked grammar, usage, and mechanics?	☐	☐
15. Have I checked spelling?	☐	☐

25

GED PRACTICE FOR SECTIONS V TO VII

To test your understanding of English and your ability to write, the GED gives you real-life situations. In other words, our day-to-day writing problems are not neatly arranged as isolated sentences in exercises in which we're watching for comma splices or pronoun errors. Rather, we face writing situations in which we must first recognize and then correct our own errors.

The GED Writing Skills Test is made up of paragraphs in which there are errors—all kinds of errors. Your task is to recognize and correct these errors. You have already worked through an earlier GED practice (Chapter 14), but this one focuses on the material in Sections V to VII. When you finish, check your answers, think through the incorrect answers, and then review rules that caused you difficulty. With that kind of preparation, you should do well on the test.

SAMPLE PRACTICE TEST

Directions: Choose the *one best answer* to each item. Items 1 to 10 refer to the following paragraph.

(1) The national physical fitness fad profits health clubs, exercise gyms, and fitness centers. (2) There is no question that fitness is important to good health. (3) The experts agree. (4) Some people, however, seemed to have the misunderstanding that fitness can result only from paid experiences. (5) They pay membership fees to sweat and feel pain. (6) They buy expensive outfits in order to be properly attired. (7) They may even buy at-home equipment seeking to maximize their time: weights, a stationary bicycle, and videos. (8) Meanwhile, the yard grows up in weeds. (9) Therein lies the irony. (10) Our parents and grandparents stayed physically fit and at the same time accomplished something. (11) They mowed the grass, trimmed the shrubs, pulled the weeds. (12) Tended the garden, scrubbed the walls, cleaned the carpets, ironed the clothes, and washed the car. (13) The exercise cost them nothing but kept them physically fit. (14) Perhaps they need to be reminded, taking lessons, and to rethink their spending priorities.

1. Sentence 1: The national physical fitness fad profits health clubs, exercise gyms, and fitness centers.

   If you rewrote sentence 1 beginning with

   Health clubs, exercise gyms, and fitness centers are

   the next words should be

   (1) national physical fitness fads
   (2) profits of national physical fitness fads
   (3) profiting from the national physical
   (4) profits from the national physical
   (5) physical fitness fad profits

2. Sentences 2 and 3: There is no question that fitness is important to good health. The experts agree.

   The most effective combination of sentences 2 and 3 would include which of the following groups of words?

   (1) Although the experts agree that
   (2) Experts agree that fitness
   (3) Because experts agree that there is no question

   (4) Good health is no question
   (5) There is no question that experts agree

3. Sentence 4: Some people, however, seemed to have the misunderstanding that fitness can result only from paid experiences.

   What correction should be made to this sentence?

   (1) Change *result only* to *only can result*.
   (2) Omit the commas before and after *however*.
   (3) Change *can* to *could*.
   (4) Replace *seemed* with *seem*.
   (5) No correction is necessary.

4. Sentences 5 and 6: They pay membership fees to sweat and feel pain. They buy expensive outfits in order to be properly attired.

   The most effective combination of sentences 5 and 6 would include which of the following groups of words?

   (1) membership fees and buy
   (2) feel pain and be properly attired
   (3) pain as well as to sweat
   (4) feel pain but buy
   (5) feel pain, therefore they buy

5. Sentence 7: They may even buy at-home equipment seeking to maximize their time: weights, a stationary bicycle, and videos.

   What correction should be made to this sentence?

   (1) Omit the colon after *time*.
   (2) Insert a comma after *equipment*.
   (3) Move *seeking to maximize their time* to the beginning of the sentence.
   (4) Change *stationary* to *stationery*.
   (5) No correction is necessary.

6. Sentences 8 and 9: Meanwhile, the yard grows up in weeds. Therein lies the irony.

   The most effective combination of sentences 8 and 9 would include which of the following groups of words?

   (1) weeds; and therein
   (2) weeds, and therein
   (3) weeds, therein
   (4) weeds, because therein
   (5) weeds, but therein

7. Sentence 10: Our parents and grandparents stayed physically fit and at the same time accomplished something.

   What correction should be made to this sentence?

   (1) Change *Our* to *Their*.
   (2) Replace *accomplished* with *accomplishing*.
   (3) Insert a comma after *fit*.
   (4) Change *stayed* to *have stayed*.
   (5) No correction is necessary.

8. Sentences 11 and 12: They mowed the grass, trimmed the shrubs, pulled the <u>weeds. Tended</u> the garden, scrubbed the walls, cleaned the carpets, ironed the clothes, and washed the car.

   Which of the following is the best way to write the underlined portion of these sentences? If you think the original is the best way, choose option (1).

   (1) weeds. Tended
   (2) weeds; tended
   (3) weeds, and tended
   (4) weeds, tended
   (5) weeds; but tended

9. Sentence 13: The exercise cost them nothing but kept them physically fit.

   What correction should be made to this sentence?

   (1) Insert a comma after *nothing*.
   (2) Change *cost* to *costed*.
   (3) Change *kept them* to *kept us*.
   (4) Replace *kept* with *keeps*.
   (5) No correction is necessary.

10. Sentence 14: Perhaps they need to be reminded, taking lessons, and to rethink their spending priorities.

    What correction should be made to this sentence?

    (1) Insert a comma after *Perhaps*.
    (2) Change *they* to *we*.
    (3) Change *need* to *needed*.
    (4) Replace *taking lessons* with *to take lessons*.
    (5) No correction is necessary.

ANSWERS

1. Correct: **(3)** The progressive form of the verb shows ongoing action. See Chapter 19, Problem 1.

   Incorrect answers: (1) To use *are* as a linking verb to connect *clubs, gyms, and centers* to *fads* changes the meaning of the sentence. See Chapter 2, Step 3, and Chapter 16, Problem 2. (2) Here the verb *are* is a helping verb and needs an *-ing* or *-ed* form of the verb to follow logically. See Chapter 19, Problem 1. (4) See item 2 above.

2. Correct: **(2)** The completed sentence should read "Experts agree that fitness is important to good health." See Chapter 16, Problem 2.

Incorrect answers: (1) To begin with an introductory word that starts an adverb clause is to create a fragment. See Chapter 8, Part 3, and Chapter 16, Problem 6. (3) See item 1 above. (4) The sentence cannot be completed logically with this beginning. (5) *There is no question* does not talk about *experts agree*; it talks about *that fitness is important*. See Chapter 16, Problem 3.

3. Correct: **(4)** The writer needs the present tense to be consistent. See Chapter 19, Problem 1.

Incorrect answers: (1) The word *only* modifies *from paid experience*, not *can result*. See Chapter 16, Problem 3. (2) *However* is an interrupter and needs commas to set it off. See Chapter 9, Rule 6. (3) *Can* is present tense and consistent with other verbs in the passage. See Chapter 19, Problem 1.

4. Correct: **(1)** The combined sentence should read, "They pay membership fees and buy expensive outfits in order to be properly attired to sweat and feel pain." See Chapter 16, Problem 2.

Incorrect answers: (2) The combination seems to omit *they buy expensive outfits*. (3) The compound parts do not reflect the two ideas in the sentences. See Chapter 15, Part 2. (4) *But* is illogical. See Chapter 15, Part 2.

5. Correct: **(3)** The participial phrase is not placed next to the word it talks about: *they*. The revision should read, "Seeking to maximize their time, they may even buy at-home equipment: weights, a stationary bicycle, and videos." See Chapter 16, Problem 3.

Incorrect answers: (1) The colon correctly means "explanation following." See Chapter 10, Part 2. (2) The participial phrase is misplaced, so a comma will not solve the problem. See Chapter 9, Summary. (4) *Stationary* is correct. See Chapter 13.

6. Correct: **(2)** To correctly join two sentences, use a comma and a joining word. See Chapter 15, Part 2.

Incorrect answers: (1) The semicolon is incorrect with a joining word and no other punctuation. See Chapter 10, Part 1, and Chapter 15, Part 2. (3) It is incorrect to join two sentences with only a comma. See Chapter 15, Part 2, and Chapter 16, Problem 5. (4) *Because* introduces an adverb clause, an illogical choice here. See Chapter 8, Part 3.

7. Correct: **(1)** The point of view has been third person. *Our* is a switch to first person. See Chapter 19, Problem 2.

Incorrect answers: (2) The progressive form of the verb is inconsistent with other verbs. See Chapter 19, Problem 1. (3) No comma is needed to join two verbs. See Chapter 2, Compound Parts, and Chapter 15, Part 2. (4) The perfect tense is not consistent with other verbs. *Stayed*, the past tense, is correct. See Chapter 19, Problem 1.

8. Correct: **(4)** The sentence is a series of balanced phrases. The comma is correct to separate items in a series. See Chapter 9, Rule 1, and Chapter 16, Problem 4.

Incorrect answers: (1) The second group of words is a sentence fragment. See Chapter 16, Problem 6. (2) A semicolon cannot separate items in a series unless the series is complicated. See Chapter 10, Part 1. (3) The *and* is illogical to separate many items in a series.

9. Correct: **(5)** The sentence is correct.

Incorrect answers: (1) No comma is needed to separate compound verbs. See Chapter 2, Compound Parts, and Chapter 15, Part 2. (2) The past tense of *cost* is *cost.* (3) *Kept them* is the third-person point of view, consistent with the rest of the passage. *Kept us* is the first-person point of view. See Chapter 19, Problem 2. (4) The past tense of *keep* is consistent with other verbs in the passage. See Chapter 19, Problem 1.

10. Correct: **(4)** To write balanced phrases, use the series of three infinitives: *to be reminded, to take lessons,* and *to rethink their spending priorities.* See Chapter 16, Problem 4.

Incorrect answers: (1) *Perhaps* is not an introductory element and so requires no comma. See Chapter 9, Rule 5. (2) The passage is in the third-person point of view. *We* is the first-person point of view. See Chapter 19, Problem 2. (3) The present tense is consistent with other verb tenses in the passage. See Chapter 19, Problem 1.

VIII

THE GED ESSAY

26
WRITING THE GED ESSAY

As you know by now, a portion of the GED Writing Skills Test is an essay response. The writing that you must do on that part of the test will be in response to a statement. You will be asked to write something like the following:

explain how to do something:

  how to control stress
  how to get along with people
  how to vote intelligently

explain why (causes or effects):

  why people litter (causes)
  why the environmental issue is important (effects)
  why we should eat and exercise properly (effects)

state and support an opinion:

  about minimum wages
  about civil rights
  about single parenting

show the advantages and/or disadvantages:

  of television programming
  of working nights
  of having children

PART 1: PLANNING YOUR RESPONSE

You have already studied how to develop each of these four kinds of responses. (See Chapters 21–24.) When you face the real test situation, however, you need a plan that will help you be successful. You have only forty-five minutes to write your response (usually of about 200 words) to the essay portion of the GED test. Knowing that, some GED applicants rush into the task without taking time to think or plan. That can be a bad mistake.

Instead, use the SLOW approach:

S - Study the question.
L - List your ideas.
O - Organize your ideas.
W - Write your statement of purpose.

Let's think through the SLOW approach one step at a time. Remember that you will have forty-five minutes to prepare your essay response. Plan to use four or five minutes to apply the SLOW Plan. We will use the following sample question to work through the steps and complete a model response:

Sample Essay Topic:

Youth looks forward to being older, more mature, able to do everything promised for "when you're older." As the young grow older, however, they often reminisce about the joys of youth.

What do you think are the advantages or disadvantages of being twenty-five? Look forward or reflect back to give specific details to support your position.

Step 1: <u>Study</u> The Question.

You will probably be a little nervous when you first read the question, worried about whether you will have anything to say, worried about whether you can write an effective response. That's natural. So take a deep breath and think carefully.

Ask yourself:

- What am I supposed to do?
  (I'm supposed to explain advantages or disadvantages. I've noticed that the directions say advantages *or* disadvantages, not advantages *and* disadvantages. So I am supposed to explain only one idea.)

 Remember: You will get no credit for responding to anything other than what the essay topic asks.

- What directions are included?
  (I am told to "give specific details." That means I must be sure to use examples that *show* advantages or disadvantages, not just tell about them.)
- How many things am I being asked to do?
  (Just one—to explain either advantages or disadvantages of being twenty-five years old.)

 Hint: Some essay topics may ask you to do *two* things. For instance, you may be asked to explain *both* advantages and disadvantages. Be sure to read the directions carefully!

Step 2: <u>List</u> The Ideas You Will Include.

For the question above, for instance, you first must decide whether to talk about advantages or disadvantages. Let's say you choose disadvantages. With that decision made, you're ready to list ideas.

Use a piece of scratch paper to write your notes. Write just key words about what you think you will include in your response to the topic.

Ask yourself:

- What do I want to say?
  For the question above, for instance, your list may look like this:

  Disadvantages of being twenty-five
  lack work experience
  too old to act like kid
  too young to fit in at work
  have lots of energy

- Have I included any ideas that do not belong?
  (Yes. Having lots of energy is not a disadvantage.)

  Revised list:

  Disadvantages of being twenty-five
  lack work experience
  too old to act like kid
  too young to fit in at work

- Do I have enough ideas for a paper?
  (Yes. Three ideas, each with examples, will be adequate to support your response.)

- What details will I use to explain each of my ideas?

 Remember: To let your reader see the picture, you must *show*, not *tell* about your subject.

Your list of details may look something like this:

lack work experience

> only four years' experience
> only two positions
> others (older) have more and different

too old to act like kid

> others my age married
> singles scene too late (work early)
> other responsibilities (yard, apartment)

too young to fit in at work

> others older, married, children, grandkids
> active in sports (they're couch potatoes)

With two or three examples to support each idea, you are ready for the next step.

Step 3: <u>Organize</u> Your Ideas

You have already studied three ways to organize ideas: time order, space order, and orders of importance. You will need to choose the best way to put your list in order. Ask yourself:

- Is there a reason to use time order or space order?

Hint: If there is no reason to use time or space order, then you will use the most frequently used order: order of importance.

• How can I organize these ideas by importance?

Disadvantages of being twenty-five

lack of work experience (most important disadvantage)
too old to act like a kid (second most important)
too young to fit in at work (least important)

 Hint: Remember that usually the most effective way to organize your ideas is from second most important to most important. As a result, the ideas above should go in this order:

    1. too old to act like a kid
    2. too young to fit in at work
    3. lack work experience

Number in order the items on your scratch list.

• In what order should I give my examples?

 Hint: Again, review the three ways to organize. Then simply use letters to put the examples in order.

    3. lack work experience
      b. only four years' experience
      a. only two positions
      c. others (older) have more and different
    1. too old to act like kid
      b. others my age married
      a. singles scene too late (work early)
      c. other responsibilities (yard, apartment)
    2. too young to fit in at work
      a. others older, married, kids, grandkids
      b. active in sports vs. couch potatoes

Step 4: <u>Write</u> the Statement of Purpose

When you write your statement of purpose, you make yourself—and your reader/evaluator—see clearly your main idea. In this example, your main idea is, of course, that there are disadvantages to being twenty-five years old. So your statement of purpose might read like this:

Statement of Purpose: The three disadvantages to being twenty-five years old make me wish I were closer to thirty-five.

Or, another version:

Statement of Purpose: At twenty-five a person is too old to act as he feels but too young to fit in at work or to have enough experience for a better job.

Or, another vetsion:

Statement of Purpose: At twenty-five a person spends frustrating days thinking, "If only I were thirty-something."

In each case, the statement or purpose says or implies the following:

1. The writer is twenty-five—or recalls being twenty-five.
2. The writer sees age twenty-five as a disadvantage.
3. The writer will detail why it is a disadvantage to be twenty-five.

Now you're ready to write. Just remember to follow the SLOW method to prepare:

S - Study the question.
L - List your ideas.
O - Organize your ideas.
W - Write your statement of purpose.

If you take the time to plan, you will write a far better essay.

PART 2: WRITING YOUR ESSAY

Now you're ready to write. If you have worked according to schedule, you should have spent four or five minutes planning. That leaves forty minutes. You will want to save time at the end for checking your paper and making some revisions—at least six or seven minutes. That leaves thirty-three minutes to write:

5 minutes planning
33 minutes writing
7 minutes checking
45 minutes total

If you have thirty-three minutes to write and three ideas to cover, then you should spend eleven minutes on each topic:

11 minutes on "too old to act like a kid"
11 minutes on "too young to fit in at work"
11 minutes on "too young to have work experience"
33 minutes on writing time

Use your thirty-three minutes this way:

Step 1: Start with the Statement of Purpose.

Use the statement of purpose as an introduction. Why? Three reasons:

1. By starting with the statement of purpose, you force yourself to say exactly what you are going to do in your essay.
2. You have already written the statement of purpose (from the planning steps above), so you can jump right into the writing task.
3. By starting with the statement of purpose, you tell your reader exactly what you are going to do in your essay.

Step 2: Write about Your Ideas in the Order in Which You Numbered and Lettered Them Above.

Writing the essay should be almost like following a road map. You know where you must go, and your planning notes tell you the steps to take to get there. So go! Get your ideas down as quickly as possible. You can puzzle over punctuation, spelling, or a precise word later.

Step 3: Add a Conclusion

The conclusion, as you remember, is a simple summary or statement to help the reader feel a sense of completeness. Keep it short and snappy. Don't waste time here.

PART 3: CHECKING YOUR ESSAY

Checking takes two steps. Remember, you should have about seven minutes to check. Use it this way:

4 minutes to check content
3 minutes to check spelling, mechanics, etc.
7 minutes total checking time

Here's how:

Step 1: Use the S2C3 Plan To Check Content.

S2C3 is just a little trick to help you remember the important things you have studied about writing. You know about them, and you'll want to remember them as you check your essay response. The letters stand for five important ideas:

S - Specific details
S - Sentence structure
C - Connecting words
C - Conclusion
C - Consistency

Ask yourself:

• Have I included *specific details*? Did I show, not tell?
• Have I used good *sentences*? Have I used a variety of sentences? Have I omitted sentence errors like run-on sentences, comma splices, and fragments?
• Have I used *connecting words* to move from one idea to the next smoothly?
• Did I add a *conclusion*?
• Did I use *consistent* verb tenses and the same point of view throughout?

Step 2: Use the GUMS Plan To Check Details.

Again, GUMS is just a little trick to help you remember to check for:

G - Grammar
U - Usage
M - Mechanics
S - Spelling

MODEL

The following essay responds to this question:

What do you think are the advantages or disadvantages of being twenty-five. Look forward or reflect back to give specific details to support your position.

The model essay that follows is based on the plan outlined above. Furthermore, since the GED Writing Skills directions usually suggest an essay of about 200 words, this model falls within the suggested length. Study the model and the marginal notes to the left. Then use the topics at the end of this chapter to practice writing your own response.

Twenty-Five or Thirty-Something?

statement of purpose, notes "three disadvantages"

Three disadvantages to being twenty-five years old make me wish I were thirty-five.

connecting word, introduces first disadvantage

First, as a young single, I would like to do what I did at eighteen, but I'm too old.

first example showing one disadvantage

The late-night scene interferes with my early-morning work assignment.

second example

My friends are almost all married, and I feel silly doing alone the things we used to do together. And

third example

since I have a yard and an apartment to keep up, I can't act like a kid anymore, ignoring responsibilities.

connecting sentence, introduces second disadvantage

It seems strange that while I'm too old for the activities of my youth, I'm too young for comfort at

connecting word, introduces first example to explain second disadvantage

work. For instance, I'm too young to fit in with my fellow workers. All of them

details

are at least thirty, married, have children, even grand-

second example

children. They tease me about my youth, mostly

details explaining why

because I like to play a fast game of racket ball, tennis, or basketball. They prefer to watch any sport for any number of hours from the

connecting word for summary

connecting sentence intro-
    ducing third disadvantage
third disadvantage

first example to explain
    third disadvantage

connecting words to introduce
    details

connecting words to introduce
    more details

connecting word to show
    results

concluding statement

living room couch. In short, we have practically nothing in common.

The biggest disadvantage to being twenty-five, however, is not social. Young adults simply cannot have the work experience to move up the success ladder. Because my fellow workers are older than I, they are also more experienced. For instance, since I have held only two positions with my employer, I am told that I lack the understanding needed for a better job. In addition, since I have only four years' experience, I am the new man on the crew. Therefore, when a position opens, someone else always has more experience than I and beats me to the promotion. Being twenty-five often leaves me wishing I were thirty-something.

PRACTICE

Use the following topics to practice preparing GED essay responses. Aim for essays of about 200 words. Time yourself so you will get used to watching the clock and preparing an essay within the forty-five-minute limit.

Sample Topic 1

Internationally, people are voicing concern over environmental issues, like air and water pollution, the depletion of natural resources, and the extinction or endangerment of many plant and animal species.

Explain how an individual can alter his or her living habits to protect the environment. Give specific details and examples to support your explanation.

Sample Topic 2

Athletes in the United States enjoy high visibility and enormous salaries. Their images fill the television screen; their contracts are topics of general discussions. As a result, many children admire athletes as heroes and turn to them as role models.

Do you view this admiration as good or bad? State your opinion and give reasons to support your position.

Sample Topic 3

Credit cards provide the convenience of buying now and paying later. On the other hand, some people are caught up in the spending power that credit cards give them, and they destroy themselves financially.

Explain why you think credit cards are good or bad. Be sure to give specific reasons and examples to support your explanation.